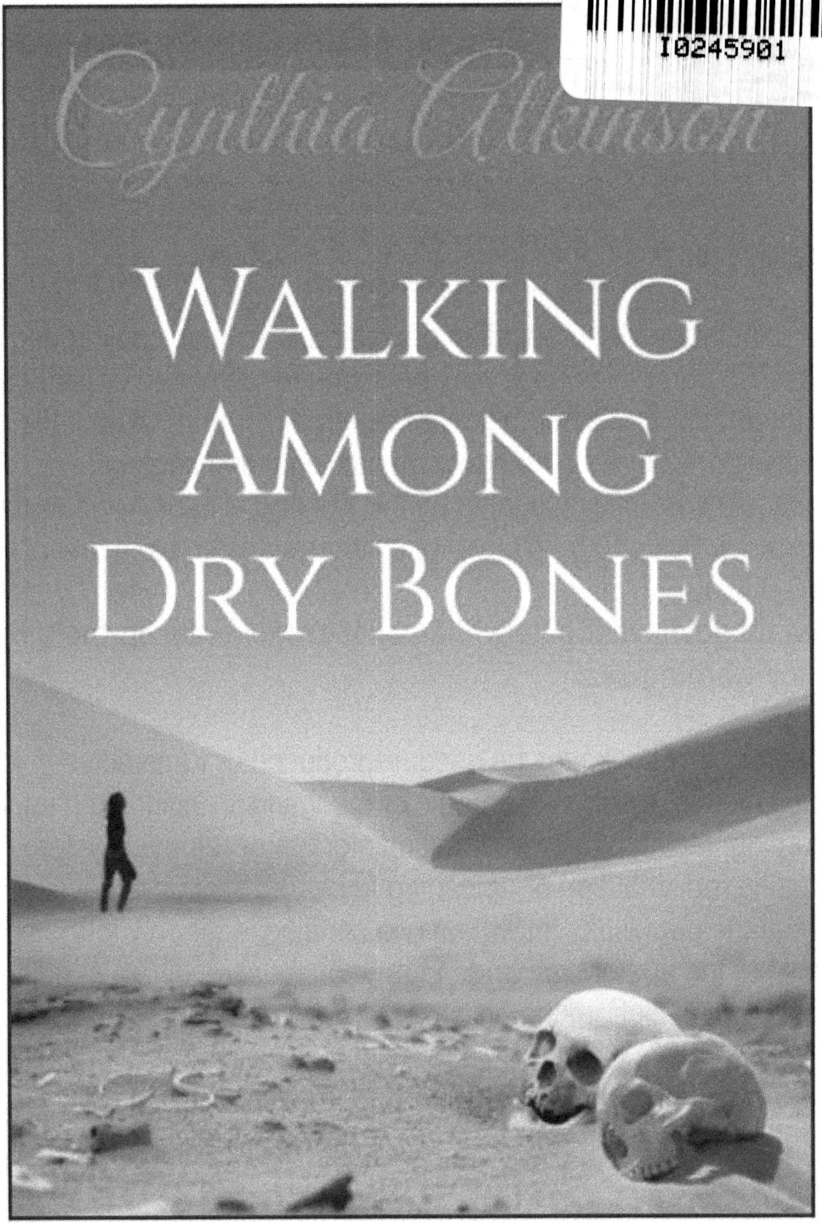
Cynthia Atkinson
WALKING
AMONG
DRY BONES

Author – Cynthia Atkinson

The Crown And Cross Consulting And Publishing Co LLC

Initial edits (2021) completed by Lady Lisa Dangerfield

Copyright © 2022 ~ The Crown And Cross Consulting And Publishing Co LLC

All Rights Reserved

Originally printed in the United States of America

The unauthorized reproduction or distribution of this copyrighted work is illegal. No part of this book may be scanned, uploaded or distributed via the internet or any other means of electronic or print without the Author's permission. Copyright infringement has legal and criminal consequences, is investigated by the FBI and is punishable under federal law by up to 5 (five) years in federal prison and a fine of $250,000.00
www.fbi.gov/investigate/white-collar-crime/piracy-ip-theft/fbi-anti-piracy-warning-seal

No part of this book may be used, reproduced or transmitted in any form or any means, electronic, graphic or mechanical, including photocopy, recording, taping by any information storage or retrieval system including redistribution or uploading to shared files or retrieval system, without the permission in writing (via certified letter only to the address below) to the author only **and** in turn, you must receive a certified letter of approval back from the below:

The Crown And Cross Consulting And Publishing Co LLC
Attention: Kimberly Stratton
PO Box 952607
Lake Mary, FL 32795

ISBN: 979-8-9853754-8-0

Intentionally blank page

In memory of my loving Mother

Bertha Mae Atkinson August 23, 1919 – July 1, 2016

My family said goodbye to our sweet Mother on July 1, 2016, a little more than a month shy of her 97th birthday. As I sat at my laptop, one year after her passing, I thought to myself that this marks the day that would've been her 98th birthday and one of the reasons I have finished this project is because of her words of knowledge.

During those last days that she was beginning her transition into her new life with our Father in Heaven, I had put my other two projects on hold and they lay dormant.

The reason for the other books being set aside was because a new book was being birthed in me during the time that my Mother was in physical rehabilitation, just before hospice, from which she would not return. I knew the Father wanted me to finish this project first.

As I sat in my Mother's hospital room, visions of this book **Walking Among Dry Bones** dropped into my spirit. I began writing what I heard that day on a small pad I had pulled from my bag. Mommy said, *"What are you writing now? You are always writing."* I laughed as I said, *"Well I got it from you; you have been writing all of my life and even before that Mommy."* We laughed.

I then told her that I had just gotten an idea for a book; telling her what I was envisioning about it. She said, *"Another one?"* Then she stated the most profound truth, she told me that I needed to finish this book, *"and then you can finish all that other writing you were doing before."* It was as if she just took my thoughts from my head because I knew I needed to get this book done first (this was confirmation). Mom knew my heart for the youth and even though she wasn't saying much else, it was when she said, "And then you can finish all that other writing you were doing before" that just stood out to me as a word of knowledge. I said, *"you know what Mommy? I'm going to finish this book first and I will dedicate it to you."*

Thank you, Mom, for not only encouraging me to be a finisher but also inspiring me to be the woman of God that I am today. I can only strive and hope to be as much of an inspiration to my own children and to the youth of today, as you were to me.

Congratulations Lady Bertha, you finished strong!

Dedication

I dedicate this book to The Most High God, my Father, Isaiah, and my Mother, Bertha, because without them none of this would have been possible. The Most High used them to inspire me to be a true woman of God. In her latter days, God used my Mom to inspire me to finish this project.

To my sister **Lisa D "Baby Dit"** for believing in me and giving me that extra push when I needed it. What a blessing you've always been to me, Phoos (insider)

All praise to my savior, Christ Jesus, my rock ... for granting me the gift of writing and imagination. Most of all, I am truly thankful for love and guidance through this project that was downloaded into my spirit directly from His Throne room, in the confines of my secret place. This is truly EPIC for me!

Friends and family ... thanks to all of you who have encouraged me and given advice through my difficult stages during this project. Of course, if I mention everyone, I'd have quite a few more pages, so I'll mention some key players.

Caitlin ... you were there from the beginning through the end; always softly interjecting edit ideas and urging me to go forward. My wonderful young friend, you're more precious as time goes on. You really ROCK. I miss you girl.

My sister twin ☺ **Jan C** (and BIG brother) **Dave C ...** ☺ thank you for reading and critiquing my many writings even when I was a total pain asking what you thought. You guys really hung in with me. Love You!

Prophetess Tara H ... no words can begin to express how I feel about you and our sisterhood. You prayed and interceded. You were always there for me; up or down. Thank you for the encouragement. I thank the Most High for you. Love you girl. #BloodCouldn'tMakeUsCloser

Apostle LaForest "Shellie" J ... you knew the gift was there. Thank you for believing in me, giving me that extra push and reminding me that I could do it in Christ's strength but mostly for the opportunity to write articles for your WEWN Newsletter. You are a true blessing.

Hunter T ... You are a treasure in my life and you have been since the very first time I met you. May you be blessed 100-fold for every blessing you stood by me and were an anchor many times for this project. Thanks for encouraging me. I'm so glad God sent you into my life and may He continue to enrich you with all goodness, grace and mercy!

There are so many others who encouraged me: Sisters **Eilene G. and Angelia K; to a special sister Carolyn F. Also, to my adult children: Andrae, Marc and Kristeena.**

I can't begin to express the entire list of people to thank because it would go on and on. I lovingly say, thank you all explicitly and may the blessings of The Most High God always flow to and upon you mightily and abundantly.

Table of Contents

Introduction 11

Hope for a future "Plan A" 13

1. Walking Among Dry Bones 15

2. Battles 23

3. Rescue 27

4. Warriors 34

5. Princes 40

6. Princesses 45

7. Challenges 50

8. Time: moving forward 57

9. Grace: Salvation is on the way 67

10. Victory 70

11. Conscience 73

12. Awakening 91

13. Calling Out 95

14. Discoveries 108

15. Shepherding 116

16. Prophesying 123

17. Miracles 129

18. No More Dry Bones 132

Table of Contents cont'd

Epilogue	142
God's Grace Abounds / Prayer	150
To my Dear Readers	151
About the Author	153
About The Publishing Co	155
Notes	156

Introduction

Plan A

This story is a portrayal, inspired by different events that have happened either in the author's own life or in the lives of people she has met. She has worked with different youth in juvenile facilities and had some one-on-one experiences, not necessarily in a professional capacity, but in more personal everyday life situations. She continues to have a heart for young people everywhere because of their own enormous plights. Just thinking back upon her own childhood, the author can't even begin to imagine being a young person today trying to make it in a world that is as corrupt as it is. She sees the young people of today as Ezekiel saw the dry bones in that valley of old when the Most High spoke to him and told him how to compel the bones to live again (**Ezekiel 37:1-14).**

The main character in this book is Victoria Hutchinson. She has experienced and is still experiencing some difficulties in her own life. Her rocky past and now very close and intimate relationship with Christ causes her to be sensitive to, and see with her heart, the things that are going on in the spirit realm with principalities and powers. In her relationships with the different young people, Victoria realizes that her battle for all their souls is a very spiritual battle as well as a natural one. She knows that she must constantly stay in prayer and not become distracted by her personal obstacles that come to challenge her determination to be victorious in this quest.

The author doesn't dwell on the character Victoria and her past. Instead, she lets the readers have brief but detailed peeks into a limited amount of Victoria's past and present world. The reason for this is to keep her audience more focused on the lives of the young people and how very similar the fictional characters are to the real lives of young people who cross our paths daily. She hopes that through this book, readers will take a closer, less judgmental second look at our youth of today rather than ignoring and avoiding them.

Not every young person today has such explosive events happening in their lives; however, the writer believes that each of our youth knows or knows of at least one other young person in or around their circle, who is having the same or similar challenges as the young people in this book. Optimistically, this book will help adults to try a bit harder to understand why the young people of this generation seem to be so "rough around the edges."

We live in a world this younger generation doesn't understand; a world that has taught them little to nothing about the real Savior who is able to help them make it through all the muck and mire so that they can come into an understanding of who they are and whose they are. So that they can understand the true plan our Father has for their lives – which is **"Plan A"**.

Hope for a future "Plan A"

The caterpillar was born to fly but he didn't know it. He thought and saw himself as insignificant and ordinary. He only saw his ugly color and lowly state. He didn't know why he was alive but he continued to crawl in spite of it all. He crawled through the rain; he crawled through the storms; he even crawled through the threat of drowning and being stepped upon.

One day he was compelled to crawl up a tree and into a dark blanket. Not knowing why he was in the blanket, he struggled to get out. He continued to struggle until a sliver of light shone through the dark blanket. The little caterpillar was so intrigued by the light that he continued to struggle until the light became brighter and brighter.

At last, he was free of the dark blanket but he noticed something was very different in the light. To his wondrous amazement, he was no longer crawling but he was flying and he was beautiful. Yes, the caterpillar was now a butterfly!! He was "born to fly" but he didn't know until he came into the light where he was able to spread his wings.

The moral of the story is to never think that you are insignificant and ordinary. Keep moving toward God's light until you can spread your wings where you shall find the real beauty you were destined to be ~ *C. E. Atkinson.*

Jeremiah 29:11 - For I know the plans that I have for you, says the Most High, plans of peace and not of evil, to give you a future and a hope.

Intentionally blank page

Chapter 1 - Walking Among Dry Bones

'Victoria imagined that he was garbed in some type of ancient black and gray vesture and his name was FEAR. She knew because he proudly wore the name displayed in a type of sequence across his chest.'

"Then I will give them one heart, and I will put a new spirit within them, and take the stony heart out of their flesh, and give them a heart of flesh"
Ezekiel 11:19.

"Wow, it's so cold out here," Victoria Graham-Hutchinson mused as she walked from her car to the building. "That's one of the reasons I really don't come here. It's cold and it's a long walk," she said aloud (why couldn't this orientation have been held in the church auditorium?). She prayed in a low but audible voice, "Father please help me. I'm not even sure what it is I'm suppose to say to them. I don't even know why I was chosen for this assignment but You know Abba." As she continued her trek uphill to the large building that seemed to be hulking over the rest of the nearby structures, she thought to herself, "I wonder why the parking area is so far from the building. Oh, just stop it with the complaining Victoria, you know better," she scolded herself out loud.

Victoria had awakened earlier than usual this morning. She felt a strong discerning within herself to pray. It was so strong that she wasn't even tempted to turn over for a few more minutes of sleep. Instead, she looked up eyes wide open, "What is it, Father?" she asked aloud. As she swung her feet over the side of the bed, she began praying in the Spirit but before her feet hit the floor she heard within her spirit, "Fear not." Immediately Victoria fell to her knees and began her morning prayer when she heard the voice again say, "Stand up, this is WAR!" As she stood, heart pounding she went back to praying in the Spirit which was so forceful that her breathing became somewhat labored. Calling upon the Holy Spirit to breathe for her, she felt her breath then become more even and she was able to continue. She continued in a type of mock march around her apartment praying on her own with such fierceness that she barely recognized her voice as her normal voice. She knew her helper was walking alongside guiding the prayer. As the tone of prayer mellowed into worship, Victoria found herself singing songs of victory as she called for the parts of her armor one by one. She smiled thinking out loud, "I can almost imagine those parts falling upon me like a Christian rendition of Iron Man." Ending the prayer battle session, she headed for the shower still singing praise songs and pondering the "fear not" warning she had heard. As she thought about it, she said aloud, "Well Abba. You know."

Once outside she got into her 10-year-old Mercury Sable, which had been so reliable for her, she thanked Elohim for her "Warrior Deborah" (the name which she happily referred to her car as). This car to Victoria was like in the Bible, a warrior. She thought to herself, 'She might not look like much but Father she has truly held up and boy can she go', Ok Deborah, it's Abba Father, you and I. Lets get about my Father's business," she stated out loud, with a matter-of-fact tilt to her head. She thanked The Most High God for her invisible Gladiator angels that she had commissioned out before her, put Deborah in drive and headed north toward her destination.

As she entered the building, she could discern and smelled the stench and rottenness of abuse, lust, fornication, pain, suffering and all those old familiar spirits that had begun accosting her inner spirit. She could visualize their dark shadows, beginning to run and hide underneath the folds of curtains and other objects. She again began pleading the blood of Jesus and praying in the Spirit. She also felt more of the larger familiar spirits of rage and incest, pornography and child predators began peeking from around corners of her mind. She said aloud, "I bind you foul spirits in the name of Jesus, the Son of the Most High God. I loose peace and love now in Christ's name! The blood of Jesus covers me and guardian angels surround me with a hedge of protection while I come against all of you in the name of the Anointed One, the Christ. Now be gone." In an instant, the stench and the shadows were gone.

Up the stairs she went. When she reached the top there was a long hallway before her stretching all the way to the room that she would enter. As she advanced toward the room, the closer she got, the more the foul odor of them seemed to accost her Spirit again. She realized at that moment that those horrible spirits had run right into the place where she was headed. As a slight brush of the spirit of panic breezed past her, she called out, "Oh no you don't. I resist you by the blood of the Holy One of Israel. **God has not given me a Spirit of fear, but of power, and of love, and of a sound mind!**" She quoted **2 Timothy 1:7** as she stopped for a moment checking her armor. **Helmet, check. Breastplate, check. Sword, check. Shield, check. Truth belt, check. Peace boots, check and all prayer, check.** Then picking up her pace she finally arrived at the door. As she reached for the knob she could hear an ugly horrible voice behind her growling, "You cannot and will not have them. Turn now. Turn and run while you have the chance." At that moment she began singing, "devil the blood of Jesus is against you!!!" More songs came rushing into her thoughts and proceeded from her mouth as she overcame the brief anxiety that tried her. As she then went forward she thought on the power of the Word of the Most High. Now anxiety was replaced by determination, reminding her of the overcoming verse in Revelation.

"For the accuser of our brethren, who accused them before our God day and night, has been cast down. ¹¹ And they overcame him by the blood of the Lamb and by the word of their testimony"
Revelation 12:10-11.

There was a small vestibule just outside the room. Victoria stopped and muttered another prayer calling on the Holy Spirit to help her. The voice deep inside of her spoke once again, now saying, "They are of a rebellious house, "**FEAR NOT.**" She wasn't sure at first if He meant the young people; then she decided that He must be speaking of those foul spirits that were holding them hostage. Stomach slightly quivering, her inner spirit accosted by the rotten stench of prostitution, sex trafficking, physical abuse as well as alcohol and drug abuse and all those terrorist spirits that had run ahead of her earlier. Still, she continued forward into the room. Victoria almost lurched up the toast and coffee she had eaten earlier. She visualized them. They were there. She could feel all those ugly little gnarled-faced creatures but this time they weren't hiding. They seemed to taunt her as she came to stand at the podium. When she looked toward the youth in the room, Victoria discerned the spirits taking their possessive places behind each person in the room: anger, jealousy, hatred, covetousness, worry, anxiety and others. You name it and they were there. The young people wore uncaring faces but pleading eyes said, "Can you help us?" She thought murmuring to herself, "I can do all things through Christ who strengthens me, please give me Your strength to endure." She closed her eyes momentarily. **"My strength is made perfect in weakness."** She was thinking now of **II Corinthians 12:9** and her insides were somewhat settled; however, still a bit on edge.

Victoria could visualize something big and dark moving in the shadows in the back of the room. Then all at once a large evil spirit with yellow eyes and the most horrid, disgusting, rotted teeth, stepped out of the recesses of her spiritual insight to make his presence and appearance known. She saw him as black, green and orange with yellowish teeth bared glaring at her as if to say, "who do you think you are that you should chase off my workers." Victoria saw that he was garbed in some type of ancient black and gray vesture and his name was **FEAR**. She knew because he proudly wore the name displayed in a type of sequence across his chest.

As she opened her tote to pull out her Bible, she felt that **Fear** and all his cohorts would be grimacing at the sight of it. Victoria held it up, as one would a sharp sword and declared, "Make no mistake about it, I always carry my sword." She then addressed her audience, "This, my dear sisters and brothers, is where we can find the means to fight and overcome every vile weapon that the enemy has."

> **"And He said to me, 'Son of man, can these bones live?'**
> **So I answered, 'O Father, You know'"**
> **Ezekiel 37:3.**

Victoria was looking at these poor souls and the foul spirits she had visualized just hovering around them when at that moment, she was taken aback; reminded of Ezekiel in the valley of dry bones. She could see in her spirit how these horrible, carnivorous, predator spirits seemed to have sucked the very life out of these young people who sat before her. Beloved beautiful children created in God's likeness. They had been beaten down and almost destroyed by these principalities and powers from the darkness. Beaten down by drugs, alcohol, abuse, sex slavery and every horrible thing life had handed them. So beat down that she felt as if she could see straight through to their bones; bones that looked as if the marrow that once had been flourishing with life had now been drained of all life-giving blood and nutrients. Drained to the point that they now resembled a dusty lifeless road in the desert wilderness where no rain, not even a fresh morning dew could quench the thirst that had overwhelmed it. It needed a tsunami of living water. "Abba, help," she whispered to herself.

> **"And again He said to me, 'Prophecy to these bones, and say to them, O dry bones, hear the Word of the Most High!'**
> **Thus says the Father to these bones' 'Surely I will cause breath to enter into you, and you <u>shall</u> live'" Ezekiel 37:4-5.**

As Victoria began speaking, she walked up and down the aisle; demons seemingly growling and hissing as she passed by them. They had no power to attack her because her commissioned angels of The Most High went with her. She now began feeling the power of the Holy Spirit fall upon her becoming more powerful as she walked and talked speaking and quoting scripture. She exercised her authority over darkness as she went, knowing now more than ever that her Helper was walking next to her, giving her added strength to conquer the quivering inside of her own belly and the trembling of her hands.

"The thief does not come except to steal, to kill, and to destroy" John 10:10.

Each of these young people who had signed up for the orientation and the "Come Back" program, had been abused, used and traumatized in some way. Fresh out of juvenile halls, orphanages, rehabilitation centers or foster homes, some even just out of prison. Each of them had felt helplessness but one thing they all had in common was that they had realized that they needed help from above or they would never have come here today. The only problem for them was they had no idea how to go about getting God's help. She went on to address every demon who was in the room by pleading the blood of Christ with each step she took and then went on to explain to the individuals (who were unaware of their jailers in the room) how the enemy had stolen their hopes and killed their dreams but that he could not destroy them unless they allowed him to. **"I have come that they may have life, and that they may have it more abundantly" John10:10.** Victoria told them that she had come to help them to discover how to keep themselves from being destroyed by the one who was after their eternal souls and how to live in Kingdom abundance. She further explained that if they really wanted to learn how to effectively stand up to the enemy, then they would need to sign up for their ten-week, one-on-one sessions with her to address their thoughts and needs privately (she knew the harsh reality was that it would take much longer). She then began boldly walking through to the back of the room where **Fear** stood mockingly. Now Victoria stood flat-footed, took a victorious stance, looked **Fear** in the eye and declared that every one of these problems was derived of **FEAR** and that there was no way he would keep her from telling the truth (that is in this small black book that she again held up like the sword it was meant to be). She imagined that he bared his teeth and glared at her only long enough to see one of the angels draw his sword. **Fear** shrank back in terror. At this point, Victoria had stood down her own fear, which was not so quietly harassing her as she spoke. At that moment, she visualized the angel as he commenced to slice **Fear** to shreds. Victoria then raised both hands in praise and worshiped Christ the Savior. She invited the students to line up at the podium to sign up for their sessions. The freedom-laced presence of the Holy Spirit was so powerful, that in an instant, those young people all but ran over each other getting up to the podium as their jailers seemed to shrink into the abyss of the room until a more auspicious time.

Chapter 2 – Battles

The ugly spirit was gone from the corner of Victoria's psyche but she had a suspicion that he was somewhere lurking, waiting to harass Gloria at the first opportunity.

Gloria Maria Santiago
Monday at 9:15am
Gloria breezed into Victoria's office fifteen minutes late for her appointment. "Hola Vicky, she spat out as she loudly chewed her gum. Victoria did not look up as she said, "You're late." "Ni siquiera quiero estar aqui," **(I don't even want to be here)** Gloria retorted. "Entonces, por que viniste? **(Then why did you come?)** Victoria answered. "Y por cierto, usted se dirigira a mi como Victoria, por favor!" **(By the way, you will address me as Victoria, please)** She looked up at the young girl for the first time and said, "or you will not address me at all," she added in English. Stunned by Victoria's fluent "Espanola." Gloria stepped back and smiled. "OMG! I thought you looked like you had some Latina in you girl." Gloria stated while smirking. "No Gloria, I'm not at all Latino. I am ½ African American, ¼ Native American and only God knows what else. Maybe Heinz 57 Variety but why should that matter to you if I'm here to help you? And it's ma'am not 'girl'. Now my second question is, would you like my help? Because it is totally your choice. You signed up."

Victoria was now looking straight at Gloria, a beautiful dark-haired 17-year-old soon to be eighteen in two weeks. She was a bit on the chunky side but very shapely with an exotic look. The look in this child's eyes was of worldly wisdom that was way beyond her years but there was so much pain in her eyes that it outshined her stunning natural beauty. Gloria looked at Victoria as she sat down when she noticed the Christian counselor was looking intently at her. She then lowered her eyes to the floor and said, "You should know that I'm really not that bad a person." At that, Victoria began to explain that she was not there to judge but to first assess her (Gloria's) needs and expectations and then figure out a way to help her. All of a sudden, darkness came across the girl's face as if she had been stung by a viper. She began yelling obscenities in a mix of Spanish and English altogether. It was spoken so rapidly that Victoria was stunned. She didn't understand all of it but she did hear this, "I ain't no welfare recipient. I got a job." Victoria then visualized that ugly spirit of anger lurking in the corner of her thoughts and though she didn't react negatively to the outburst, it was a bit unnerving since it seemingly came unprovoked. Gloria then began breathing hard, panting, wheezing and sweating. Victoria knew from the file that the girl was asthmatic, so she calmly asked if she had her pump with her. Gloria then began to react sadly, confused and somewhat embarrassed before the woman who spoke so kindly to her after her tirade. Still breathing heavily, she calmed herself long enough to extract the asthma pump from her jacket's pocket. Victoria then asked her if she would like a glass of water to which she nodded her head in affirmation. Victoria could now envision the angry spirit that was trying to strangle Gloria, trying to consume her every thought. "The devil is a LIAR. The blood of Jesus is against you!" Victoria said this in a low voice but forceful enough for the angel that had entered to slice the little gnarled face thing to shreds as he took flight. After a few moments and a few more sips of water, Gloria was composed and spoke again. She told Victoria that she was not a charity case and she didn't need anyone's help. Again, Victoria asked her why she came and purposefully pointed out that she (Victoria) had not intended to imply charity but was asking of Gloria's personal needs. At this point, Gloria began to cry and say, "because-... I don't want to be angry all the time but I can't help it". Victoria said some soothing words to the girl then wrote down a scripture for her. **"I can do all things through Christ, who strengthens me" Philippians 4:13.** Then she asked Gloria if she would try to memorize it by the next session. After reading the paper it was written on Gloria looked puzzled. Victoria asked if something was wrong. Gloria looked up from the paper and asked if this was true. "Well, yes, it certainly is!" Victoria said with a wide toothy grin. She was now able to use the rest of the session to explain as best she could what the scripture meant and how it worked. She also asked Gloria just as she would ask her other clients if she had ever asked Christ into her heart and then if she would meditate on the passage and prepare to discuss what it meant to her in the next session. The ugly spirit was gone from the corner of Victoria's thoughts but she had a strong suspicion that he was somewhere lurking, waiting to harass Gloria at the first opportunity.

Gloria's file read like this: her story is one of abuse at the hands of her own mother, who had beaten her from as far back as Gloria could remember. She had also dressed Gloria up and made up her face to appear older looking. Gloria's mother had her at age thirteen and while still innocent-looking, was dressed up to prostitute her underdeveloped body to grown men. Gloria was not much more than a baby herself. Her mother justified to the child that it was her fault that her lazy "Poppy" had walked out, so Gloria needed to get out and work to get milk and pampers for her baby brother. The file also stated that Gloria had an older sister named Damaris, who had run away at age sixteen but was later found beaten to death in another state. Her mother had never reported her missing; therefore, her death would never have been known by her family if it wasn't for another prostitute reporting it. She had shared a room with Damaris. The roommate identified Damaris from a composite that asked, "Do you know this girl." It was a sketch she had seen in the local newspaper. Damaris had told her roommate of her life story and her real name; otherwise, she would have been just another Jane in the long list of Doe's.

Victoria couldn't sleep that night due to images of this poor, beautiful rejected girl. At 1:00am, Victoria finally slid out of bed, fell onto her knees and prayed again for Gloria and her two younger siblings who were now in foster care. Victoria also prayed for Gloria's mom who was now in jail for stabbing her children's father who had come back to live there after Gloria had gone into foster care. Gloria's mother was sentenced to four to seven years for attempted murder. Victoria prayed for all the other clients she had seen that day and ended her prayer with **Psalm 127:2 "… for He gives sleep to his beloved."** She half-smiled at the thought of this feisty little girl calling her "Vicky". After all, Victoria had never let anyone call her Vicky, not even grammar schoolteachers. She was named after her dad Victor who had been a powerful man of prayer and whom she had always loved and admired. He had told her many times that their names were derivative of victory and that they were victorious conquerors in Christ. Victoria thought it an insult to shorten it to Vicky. She fell into a deep sleep but her dreams were of the hurting children.

Chapter 3 - Rescue

This thing had pointy teeth when it showed its twisted smile. Then she saw "deceit" written on his chest. "Hmmm," she thought looking at Caleb. "So that's it."

Caleb Jeremiah Austin
10:00am

He was a tall, handsome young man of sixteen; however, at first glance, he would easily pass for a twenty-year-old. In fact, he had more facial hair than most twenty -year-olds. Caleb was a caramel-skinned African American and Caucasian boy with a history of being a bully. He had been thrown off the football team for bullying and eventually expelled from school for excessive fighting. Eventually, he and a friend held up a convenience store. They had got away with almost $1,000.00 until his great aunt, (Aunt Kathy), who was raising him, found the gun and half of the money in his room. She put two and two together, from the description of the boys on the news, and knew immediately that it was Caleb and his no-good friend Trae. They only lived two blocks from that store. Well, she was sick of it. She had had it with his disrespectful and ungrateful ways. She had taken him in after his mother was killed in a car accident; his father was a crack addict and in jail for armed robbery and this "sorry boy" (as she always called him) had been one problem after another. She decided months ago that "Bully Caleb" was a bad influence on her own son, Brian. Besides Caleb had given Brian a black eye once and always bullied him for his allowance. Caleb always had a smile, a smart mouth and refused her when she tried to get the allowance back. He always had a good bold-faced lie as to where he had gotten 'his' money. "Well, let's just see how he'll be smiling now. No more. This was the last straw! He had to G.O. (get out) Aunt Kathy thought to herself as she picked up the phone to make a call to turn both Caleb and Trae in. The man at the store identified them but he was adamant that it was Caleb who had the gun. At fourteen years old he had an armed robbery charge. They sentenced him to juvenile prison but his time was reduced to barely any time in with several years of probation. Plus he would have an expunged record after the three years of probation were up.

The preacher (Rev. Carl) who volunteered at the Community center had asked for leniency for this troubled youngster and promised to take some responsibility for Caleb when he got out. Reverend Carl Trolli had recognized Caleb's intelligence and other abilities. He wanted to help this kid who had had so many tough breaks. The Reverend saw good in Caleb's eyes every time they talked but the child had just lost his mother and there was no dad around to help positively bring him up. Reverend Trolli had also met Aunt Kathy who was not the best role model for young Caleb. He knew that she drank daily and dibbled and dabbed in other things. A few years back when the child was a lot smaller, he had witnessed her slapping Caleb; cursing and calling him everything except his name. *"Not that his behavior should be excused but it was no wonder he bullied Brian. He had been bullied by Aunt Kathy and had learned her own angry behavior."* Reverend Trolli had argued this for Caleb to the court-appointed attorney representing the child. The Reverend had a flashback when he first met Caleb. It was the day this woman (his aunt) was slapping and cursing him. The Reverend saw him and had gone to the child after his own aunt left on the playground crying. He had soothed and calmed the child and brought him into the youth center. Caleb was intelligent and cooperative when he came to the center; always willing to help. He was interested in the Bible sessions. After that incident, he continued coming to the center. When Aunt Kathy saw how much Caleb enjoyed his time at the center, she had threatened him a few times and told him he couldn't go there anymore. Now Caleb had to sneak out to go and he told the Reverend which angered him. "Reverend (Rev.) Tee" as the kids called him, went to Caleb's house and had a visit with Aunt Kathy. She was insistently saying that Caleb couldn't go right up until Reverend Tee politely and firmly began telling her that he knew she was having problems. He casually mentioned her drug and alcohol usage and suggested she go to rehab. Aunt Kathy changed her tune really quickly. She didn't need anyone calling Child Protective Services and taking her precious Brian away. Not to mention the money she got for the "sorry boy", Caleb. "Well, I guess he can go with his sorry self." She went on about how he was never gonna amount to nothin' and he was gonna end up just like his sorry daddy. Reverend Tee stood up and walked toward the front door to leave. Once he was out of the door, he could still hear her as she went on with her drunken ranting. He was shaking his head as he heard the door slam again. He looked back and it was Caleb coming up from behind him. "I'm coming with you Reverend Tee. I don't want to get hit by no flyin' pans or any other stuff she's throwin'." Rev. Tee shook his head even more and told him that there would be a Bible session today. Caleb smiled. Rev. Tee kept watch over Caleb and had seen the boy's anger from time to time but he could also see the good in him. Sometimes he would see a sneaky side too as Caleb continued to grow up.

Caleb was prompt and already seated for his session when Victoria walked into the office. She had suffered all day with a crazy headache. She normally didn't get headaches, so this was annoying and here sat this arrogant-looking young kid slouched in the chair looking her up and down as if she were a teenager. However shapely she was, Victoria was not about to have this child looking at her in that way. Immediately, she belted out, "Sit up straight and don't look at me like that. I'm 63-years-old. I have grandsons older than you." Caleb sat up and said "yes ma'am. I'm sorry." Somewhat surprised by his response, Victoria took her seat behind her desk. When she looked up, she could see in her mind's corner a vision of a little, fuzzy, ugly teddy bear-ish creature sneering at her. This thing had yellow disgusting teeth when it showed its twisted smile. Then she saw "deceit" written on his chest. "Hmmm." she thought looking at Caleb. "So that's it." Then she said point-blank, "ok are you apologizing or are you telling me that you're 'sorry'?" He looked puzzled for a minute, then he said, "I apologize." Victoria went on to ask him what had changed his mind about saying 'I'm sorry'. Caleb told her it was because his Aunt Kathy always called him 'sorry' and some of the guards at juvie had called him 'sorry' and that had made him want to choke the life out of them. Then he said, in a quiet but deceptive tone, "but I just smiled and I was thinking of a way to get them back when I got the opportunity." "Oh and I did get that big guard. Once I was helping in the kitchen at juvie and I had seen some Ex-lax in the cabinet. Yup! I made sure that guard got a little surprise in his chocolate cake. At Caleb's words, Victoria could picture that creepy little thing in the corner of her thoughts began spinning around as if it had scored some goal or touchdown. 'So that was it'. This deceitful spirit was causing Caleb to be cunning and crafty, hiding behind a handsome smile.

Caleb's file read that he was quite intelligent with a high IQ but he refused to apply himself. He would turn in blank tests and no homework while he was in school. His teachers from grammar school said he was a good student with straight A's until his mother was killed. Then, he just went downhill from the minute he hit middle school.

"Alright Caleb," Victoria said, "I'll be straight with you. I can only help you if you are straight with me. And I'll tell you something else, it won't be easy to fool me and you definitely can't fool God. So, I would advise you to tell Him and me the truth. You have no reason to try to deceive Him because He already knows and as for me, there's no reason to fool me because you chose to come here, to help yourself. So, let's try to get started on the right foot, ok." She went on telling him that the Bible had many truths and promises for him to discover and it would be to his benefit to discover them and to apply them. She told him that his eternal soul was depending on him to be successful. Victoria knew that she could talk to this young man this way because of his level of intelligence and because Reverend Trolli had discussed with her that Caleb had been active in Bible sessions and seemed quite intrigued by it. Victoria decided to ask him what his top two goals were. She was surprised and delighted when he answered right away. He knew what he wanted to do and she discerned that he was being quite honest. He gave her good eye contact for the first time when he said, "I really want to know more about God and Christ and I want to get my GED." Victoria asked him why he thought he needed that GED. He thought for a moment and then he told her that he wanted it to show his Aunt Kathy and those guards at juvie that he wasn't "sorry" but mostly he wanted it so he would know for himself that he wasn't "sorry". Plus, if his mama was telling the truth when she said, "somebody up there loves you, Caleb. He's watching you and you are going to be successful." Then he told her he really wanted more education after he received his GED. As soon as Caleb uttered the words, Victoria visualized the large angel swoop down upon the fuzzy creature with one swipe of his sword. The creature squealed running and half flying out of the room with the angel hot on his heels. She smiled and thought to herself, "YES!"

Victoria thought that Caleb needed to memorize one of her favorite passages from the *New American Standard Bible* and it reads like this **"And though your beginning was small your latter days will be great" Job 8:7.**

Victoria knew from experience that she would have to really pray for Caleb. That ole deceitful spirit was a hard nut to crack. There were many other spirits wrapped up inside of deceit. Anger was one of them which is why Caleb had a tendency to be a bully but the big bad wolf of deceit and every other spirit is **FEAR** which had bullied Victoria for much of her young life. Oh yes, she knew it all too well. Since she had also learned at an early age how to be prideful and to put on a sweet little happy face when she needed to. It took many years and much prayer for her to learn to be herself and not to succumb to the dictates of deceit. Yes she knew this spirit all to pieces and so she knew he wasn't going anywhere without a fight. She would pray for Caleb and Gloria tonight.

As Victoria's day drew to an end, after praying, she began

reflecting on her own life and how she came to do the counseling for these young people. She had gone to college, so she had a degree in social psychology. Her thoughts took her to when she started attending Pillar and Ground of Truth church.

One day after service she went to the front of the church to talk with the speaker, who at that time was Carl Trolli Jr. After that day they began meeting regularly to talk about the young people. She reflected on how she felt so comfortable talking to him and of the kinship she felt with him. He had the same passion for the youth as she did, they even talked about her becoming the youth pastor at some point. Once she learned of the youth center, "Counseling for the Youth" dream was birthed in her spirit. She suggested it but never expected to head it up. Now here she is with twenty young people counting on her to make a difference in their lives. She also thought on how kind and supportive Carl had been through it all.

Chapter 4 - Warriors

Carl Trolli, Jr.
Carl Trolli, Jr.'s life started with meager beginnings. His Father is the Pastor of a small church with a small rector's house provided by the church as part of his salary. Most of the pastors who came before him didn't stay long because the church was small and the salary wasn't as sufficient as they wanted. However, Carlton Trolli Sr. was not one who was as interested so much in the pay as he was interested in providing sermons that taught his congregation the Bible. His wife, Constance Trolli was a woman with a heart of love for her family and people. She understood her husband's need to teach God's Word in truth. The people who attended Pillar and Ground of Truth Inter-denominational Church, were those who were hungry for Bible knowledge and took the good with the bad. "At this church teaching the truth will always be first priority," the Reverend would say and he would add, "If anyone wants the Bible sugarcoated this is not the church for you."

Carl Trolli Jr. grew up on this truth; at seventeen years old and a junior in high school, he already knew he had a call to the ministry. He had known for sure since he was twelve. He hung on the words his father taught and he read his Bible for himself. Carl Jr. had an intimate relationship with his Abba Father even at a very young age. Carl Sr. and Constance knew this about their son and the Trollis believed in letting their son make his own decisions but only with their sincere guidance. After all Carl was a good and obedient boy, he was also a good student in
school. Even though Carl Jr. knew this he tried never to do

anything to disappoint his parents or his Lord.

Standing 6 foot 5 inches tall, Carl, of course, played basketball and he was good at it. He never missed an opportunity to play a good game, mostly at the Community Center. He also was recruited to play on the varsity team at school. Most of the boys in his neighborhood were African American but there were a few Caucasian families too; since Carlton Sr. was from a mixed background of Italian and Native American and Constance was Sicilian, they were lumped in with the Caucasians when anyone was asking. Some of the boys could be a bit unsavory but for the most part, the neighborhood was good. Carl Jr. fit right in at the community center and everyone liked him, his best friend, Dave Washington, was African American and had started everyone calling Carl Jr., "Trolli." Later they shortened it to "Tee." One day as he was hanging out with some of the guys, he was in for a big surprise, a few of the troublemakers had stuffed their pockets with some things while in the store. Carl bought a soda unaware of the other guy's plans, until they were stopped at the door, the security guard searched everyone. Much to Carl and Dave's surprise they both had stolen items in their gym bags. The troublemakers had stashed items in their own bags and in Carl and Dave's bags when they weren't looking. They tried to explain but security called the police anyway; they ended up in court. The principal and teachers spoke well of Dave and Carl, so the judge was lenient with them.

Young Carl and Dave got good grades and were respectful and helpful students. The school board had always provided financial help to the Community Center and the kids went there when they needed extra help. Of course Carl's probation would be to tutor math and reading at the center. He and Dave also had cleanup duty after school three days a week for six months. None of it would go on either of their records, and the judge had stressed to them that this was a lesson to them to choose their friends more wisely. His parents believed Carl and Dave's story so they spoke with Dave's parents and no home punishment was administered for him either. All four parents reiterated to the boys to choose better friends. Carl and Dave never let those guys hang out with them again.

Mid-year, Carl began being approached and receiving calls from college recruiters because of his grades, reputation, and basketball skills he was a prime candidate for most colleges. He knew that whatever his decision, Carl Sr. and Constance would support him. He had settled on Virginia Tech, mostly because of the outstanding academics there and the scholarship they offered. Since Dave Washington was such an outstanding student, always on the honor roll he was also accepted to Virginia Tech on a full academic scholarship. Both Carl and Dave excelled there and became very well-known throughout the next four years. Carl was a star player and outstanding student; in his junior year at Virginia Tech, NBA teams began scouting him. He had many offers but his mind and heart was always the ministry.

Carl continued his schooling. He would decide later after graduating that he would take an offer from the LA Clippers, but he would also study Bible principles at every opportunity. In his first season with the Clippers he was excelling even more at basketball so much so that the Lakers were now scouting around him. He was about to accept the offer from them for the next season when he was fouled as he was going for a layup;

he hit the floor in an awkward sprawl. At the hospital, he was informed that he had a torn ACL, torn meniscus, a broken ankle and torn Achilles tendon. The prognosis was gloomy to say the least. He would walk again with therapy, maybe even play a little ball, but no way was he playing basketball professionally, ever.

Everyone he knew was telling him how sorry they were that he wouldn't play again but Carl wasn't as upset as most would be; he felt he needed more time to spend with the Father anyway. The ministry was always his main focus, it was always everyone else who were so fired up about basketball. Indeed he was a little disappointed but not crushed over the news. "With his great grades and being an accounting major, he would do well anyway", he thought to himself.

In his senior year at Virginia Tech, he had met Lori Lipscomb. She came to church service at the campus hall. Lori was also a senior who had transferred from Old Dominion University (ODU) in her sophomore year. Carl couldn't believe he hadn't seen her before, probably due to his focus on the basketball team and all the NBA offers he was receiving. He couldn't take his eyes off of her. At one point she looked over and their eyes locked for several seconds before she smiled and turned back to the minister who was speaking. Lori had noticed Carl long before that day. Carl approached Lori after class, they realized they were both from Richmond, and from then on they were an inseparable item. Dave Washington had also met the love of his life, Madison Singleton. That spring both couples graduated tops in the class, Lori was valedictorian while Carl and the others had special honors. After they moved back to Richmond, Lori was employed as a paralegal at a reputable firm soon after school was out; her intention was to further her education and career later after she saved some money. Carl & Dave, since they both were now CPAs had begun work at an accounting firm and were building a great reputation there. Years later they were able to start their own firm. They built profitable clientele with companies in and around Richmond.

Several years later Lori and Carl were married, within six months there was a baby on the way. Nine months later Carlton Trolli III arrived to a very happy couple. As years passed Lori became a lawyer, and Carl and Dave's firm was growing nicely. Carl had finished Bible principles and ordination. He continued volunteering at the Community Center after the church took it over. When Carlton III was nineteen and in college, his mother Lori was diagnosed with aggressive Leukemia. She and Carl Jr. prayed and prayed but Lori continued to decline. There were months of fighting it, with many tests, chemotherapy and radiation, sadly, Lori lost her battle with the awful blood cancer.

Carl was devastated to have lost his beloved Lori, so much so that he hadn't even thought to re-marry even after years had gone by. He had to go on living this lonely life but he would live it by faith. He continued on to become associate Pastor at Pillar and Ground of Truth Church alongside his father. Carl senior was old now and declining a bit so Carl Jr. did most of the ministry along with his son and others of the congregation. He made it his life's mission to help the youth to gain an understanding of faith in God and living a victorious life in Him.

The Community Center grew and many youth came there for activities and Bible principles. Not all of them would be successful but a good percentage of them did well, due to Carlton's dedication. The center's notoriety gained it government financial support and support from many local churches. The accounting firm continued to thrive. Carl and Dave had hired other accountants so they were both able to come to work for eight hours only sometimes, along with the necessary meetings. Dave was CEO, while Carl was CFO and Chief advisor.

One day years later after church service, Rev. Carlton Trolli Jr. met with a Christian social worker, Victoria Graham–Hutchinson. The two became very good friends which later led them to begin a collaboration to help and direct troubled youth in the community.

Chapter 5 - Princes

Victoria sensed a spirit of pride parading around the room, however, she was equally as unimpressed by the spirit. She would deal with that pride issue later.

Vincent Anthony Incorvia
11:00am

Vinnie was an Italian mix; a young man with a rugged handsomeness and a thick New York accent. A twenty-seven-year-old parolee who had seen the toughest of the mean streets of New York. He was born to a Charismatic Pentecostal preacher also named Vincent who had refused to have any part of his old family under dealings. He had gone into ministry right out of high school. Vinnie's mother, Celeste, was the product of a Pentecostal African American mother and an Italian father. She was a quiet and beautiful woman with wavy chestnut hair and bright brown eyes to match, she was a faithful intercessor, who meant business in the prayer room.

Vinnie started out as a good boy in the church and went on to become a youth Sunday school teacher at age fifteen. Some things changed and went very wrong when Vinnie made it onto the varsity football team in his freshman year of high school. He changed fast and drastically, he started following the crowd and trying to prove that he wasn't a "holy roller P.K." (Preacher's kid) as the guys would tease. He had begun smoking marijuana with some of the seniors, he would stay out late at parties getting high and worrying Celeste to tears. Vinnie was also so angry because his father was always doing something with church folks and barely ever had time for his family. He always had excuses why he couldn't come to any games. (Vinnie had actually discovered that his holier than Thou Father had been secretly seeing one of the new choir members who was young and sassy). That old hypocrite Vinnie would say under his breath. To add salt to his wounds, Vinnie was suspended from the team when he tested positive in a random drug test. He really became angry when the guys that had smoked with him, didn't get tested; he said it was a set up. This was the beginning of a cycle of blaming everyone else for his problems. He blamed teachers for his eventually dropping out of school, he blamed the coach because he kicked him off the football team and so on.

By age 19 Vinnie was taking pills and drinking, after only a few months pill popping and drinking, being kicked off the team, and dropping out of school…), he was introduced to crack cocaine, with that he went completely downhill. His mother, Celeste, continued to cry and pray while Vincent Sr. continued with church and his sordid affair. It ended up that at age twenty Vinnie was totally hooked on drugs. He started to sell crack to support his habit, after a while he got hung up on a possession charge. He spent twelve months in county lock up then he got out and went home. Vinnie was staying with his mother a short while but with her hovering over him, wailing and crying and on her knees about his dad, he just had to get out of there. He went back to the same old rut, but this time it was worse. He got arrested for a sale to an undercover narcotics agent, and when they searched him, he had more than enough drugs on him to send him away for quite a few years. Because of his mother's prayers, he got less time in prison than what it could have been.

Now recently paroled, Vinnie needed to "get myself together" as he would often say, but he didn't know how and the anger about his Father's infidelity still hovered over his head. He was supposed to be an example, but he continued to sneak around with his mistresses. He wasn't fooling Vinnie, Celeste or any of the church members. There was scandalous talk and a lot of it, so much talk that the boards at the church were setting up a meeting of intervention and possibly suspending him from being pastor at the church.

Vinnie had been weightlifting while in prison so he was muscular with quite an intimidating appearance. Victoria walked into her office; even though she saw this large man sitting there with his eyebrows knit together in what looked like a permanent frown. She seemed quite unimpressed. Victoria sensed a spirit of pride parading around the room; however, she was equally as unimpressed by the spirit. She would deal with that pride issue later. She cleared her throat and said, "Good morning Vincent. My name if you don't remember is… "Vinnie", he interrupted. Victoria didn't miss a beat, "No sir, my name is not Vinnie; my name is Victoria." Vinnie smiled, and said, "I meant my name is Vinnie." She stood just looking at him for a long moment, then she told him that she had been taught never to interrupt when someone else is speaking. She said to him that she had also learned not to acknowledge someone who had interrupted her in midsentence, "So I'd thank you not to interrupt me in the future" 'Are we clear on that?' she said, tilting her head. "Crystal," Vinnie replied, frowning even more. She went on to tell him that the card she held said that his name was Vincent, but that she would be happy to address him by Vinnie if that's what he preferred.

Victoria then began explaining to him why she didn't allow people to call her Vicky and she told him what Victoria meant. Then she asked if anyone had ever told him what the name Vincent meant. He tried to appear uninterested as he said, "Nah, I don't have the vaguest." Old Pride thought he had the upper hand but Victoria had an inkling from Vincent's body language that he was very curious, so she asked him if he would like to know what Vincent meant. At this Vinnie sat up straight and said, "Yeah, sure, but I can't believe you know." Then she told him of a quest she had gone on while researching 'V' names for a college term paper. She told him that Vincent was derived from the Roman name Vincentius, which was derived from the Latin word "Vincere" which means "to conquer." The name was popular among early Christians and that to conquer is in close relationship with victory. She also explained why in the early days, names meant a great deal to people and was believed to be significant to a person's life and their successes. "Now, wouldn't you like to live up to that name and conquer all the junk in your past?" Vinnie was on the edge of his seat, as if he was watching a major league playoff game and his favorite team was winning by a hair with only minutes left in the game. When she finished, she asked him if he still wanted her to call him Vinnie or if Vincent was ok, because she thought it was a great name and that it suited him. "Um er, Vincent, please ma'am." The prideful spirit she had sensed before, seemed to have fizzled away the moment the conquering angels came into remembrance. He replied with a new look; a look that was one of respect and admiration. They finished the session by going over other "V" names he thought of and asked about like Valerie, Vanessa and Valentina. He even asked about Vashti – the queen in the Bible who had been banished for disobeying a direct command from her husband the King, before he married Queen Esther. Well because Victoria knew what all of these names meant and what they were derived from, Vinnie was impressed, so much that the frown was gone, replaced by a look of curiosity. It was a good session and Vincent had said that he looked forward to coming back next week.

The scripture she gave Vincent to memorize was this **"In all these things, we are more than conquerors through Him that loved us" Romans 8:37**.

Tonight, Victoria would pray for Gloria, Caleb and Vincent. She still had quite a few more of these young people to meet with one on one. So she knew that judging from the three she had already spoken with today that the next ten weeks would call for much prayer and patience. "Father, help me," she prayed quietly.

Chapter 6 – Princesses

Victoria could see old man Fear himself lurking over in the demon corner of her thoughts. He wasn't nearly as big as he was that first day she had envisioned his presence looming in the room at orientation. Nonetheless, he was there.

Stephanie LaTrese Davis
1:00pm

Sassy, African American, a beautiful young woman with a body that was one that the other women envied and would pay good money to copy. Stephanie is twenty-five years old and has tried every drug she thought she was big and bad enough to try, the result being a fierce opioid addiction. Now with two children ages five and seven, Stephanie had just been through the drug rehab center. She had recently taken a job as a stripper to support her family and her drug indulgences and had also begun some afternoon classes. Stephanie had been through rehab several times before, to "kick" one drug habit or another but the Percocet addiction she just couldn't seem to shake. Stephanie wasn't really sure she even wanted to quit. She had suffered most of her life with leg pain, due to the fact that she had once jumped from the second-floor apartment, trying to get away from her two stepbrothers. But now she took those pills because she couldn't seem to function without them, there was just way too much pain.

Stephanie's father had suffered from mental illness and committed suicide when she was an infant. She had been molested and raped by her two stepbrothers every chance they got. They started molesting her at age four and the first rape occurred when she was nine and a half. Her mother worked the third shift and was always too tired to listen to her about her second deceased husband's sons. They would come after Stephanie waking her from her sleep and she had had enough. One night when she was 13 and her mother was at work, she managed to wedge a chair under the doorknob in her bedroom. When they came after her and couldn't get in they began kicking the door and yelling obscenities. Terrified and determined not to let them near her again, she opened her window and jumped out. She ran and ran but her legs hurt terribly and have ever since. She had begun taking different over-the- counter meds for pain until eventually she met Richard, who was older and had promised that her brothers would never bother her again. Rick gave her some pills that made her feel strange but they took away the pain and she slept very well, with no ugly dreams. Stephanie wasn't quite sure what he had said to those evil stepbrothers of hers but it worked. Even though they glared at her as if they hated her, they both left her alone with not even so much as those slaps on the behind that they had given her before throughout the day. Richard had promised and fulfilled his promise but had she traded two abusers for one even more demanding and fierce than the two combined?

She sat fidgeting in her chair, feeling uncomfortable as she waited for this woman to say something. What was she writing? Why wouldn't she just say something else? It seemed hours to Stephanie since the woman had said good afternoon. At last, Victoria looked up and said, "Please forgive me for taking so long to start, there have been several unexpected changes to my schedule so I needed to shift some things around." "Now let's get to why you've decided to come to see me today besides the order from court. I know this is a part of probation and you had other choices; yet, you chose to come to us." Stephanie had been caught stealing; receiving a suspended sentence and probation, she had chosen counseling as a part of her sentence.

Victoria observed that this young lady seemed uncomfortable in her own skin so she said, "I see here that you have enrolled in school to become a nail technician." "So how is that going?" "It's Ah-ight" Stephanie said, with a look that was disturbingly unconcerned.

After several seconds, Victoria asked her, if that wasn't what she wanted to do, then why was she taking the class? Stephanie looked genuinely puzzled. "What makes you think I don't want to do that", she asked. Victoria told her that it was because she seemed to not care if she took the class or not. Stephanie paused for a moment and then she said that she was trying to do something so she wouldn't have to dance anymore. "I don't want my kids growing up gettin' teased cause, 'they mama' is a stripper". "You know what I mean?" Victoria thought on this for a moment before she answered. She needed to tread lightly so as not to seem judgmental. After what had happened with Gloria earlier, she didn't need any misunderstandings or outbursts of anger. As she thought on it, from her mind's vision, Victoria could see old man **Fear** himself lurking over in the demon corner. He wasn't nearly as big as he was that first day she had envisioned his presence looming in the room at orientation. Nonetheless, he was there. That was it, Stephanie was afraid to take a step higher into her real dream of being an elementary school teacher. This was revealed to

Victoria later in the session, as she all but pried it out of the girl. Victoria knew that there was a stronger fear within this young girl, she could tell by the nervous fidgeting Stephanie continued to display.

Stephanie loved children and wanted not only to teach them reading and math; but she wanted to educate them on the predators in the world. She had the dream but lacked the confidence to go forward; she was afraid she would fail. Victoria ended the session by encouraging Stephanie and telling her not to give up on the dream. They also discussed schools and financial options. Stephanie had stopped fidgeting and had become a little more optimistic about her future. All the while Victoria was praying in her heavenly language every chance she could until the warring angel appeared. In Victoria's discerning spirit, fear had shrunk down to a minuscule little creep the size of a mouse, but she also felt that he still lingered in Stephanie's spirit just waiting to follow her out of the room. Victoria gave her a paper to memorize for the next session. For the third time today, this passage of scripture was much needed. **"I can do all things through Christ, The Anointed One, Who gives me strength" Philippians 4:13.**

As Victoria watched Stephanie leaving from the window she spied the reason that mouse-like demon followed the girl. She walked to the car where an older man was waiting for her and the moment she approached him he roughly grabbed her arm and said something in her ear. This made the thing that Victoria had perceived, grow to enormous proportions. As she imagined, it climbed into the back seat. She could almost see it looking up at the window smiling and baring decayed disgusting teeth as if he thought he had won this battle. Victoria pointed her finger and said out loud, "I know you can hear me and I'll tell you this, the war has just begun."

Tonight Victoria would pray for Gloria, Caleb, Vincent and Stephanie. "Well Abba" she mused, "We really have our work cut out for us." "Guide me Father, I know it's not by power or by might, but by your Spirit."

Chapter 7 – Challenges

The spirits that followed Aidan were old anger, bullying, and abuse. Victoria also felt that stealing and fighting was with them and you best believe that old man Fear was standing right with them over in the old demon corner.

Aiden Hunter O'Connor
2:30pm

Aidan came from an Irish background, and he had outbursts of temper and anger. Even though he was only the tender age of 14, Aidan had been in a boy's home, was thrown out and sent to juvie for stealing from another boy and then fighting him about it. He was now living with another foster family. In reading his file, Victoria thought that Aidan might be the hardest little 14-year-old she would ever encounter. She herself had come from a large family of boy cousins, not to mention two brothers of her own. Victoria had met some doozies via some of her own brother's friends, her nephews and their friends. This child Aidan was really something very different, seeming to be all whales, snails and puppy dog tails… but was he, really?

His parents had gotten married right out of high school, largely because Aidan's older brother, Paulie, was on the way into the world. Aidan had been in an orphanage because of the many circumstances he'd faced. His mother Colleen had left them after his father Paul had an affair with her so-called best friend. His mother never bothered to call to check on Aidan, saying that her second biggest mistake was having another baby when she knew her husband was a cheater. Her first biggest mistake had been marrying Paul in the first place. They fought every day and Aidan always thought it was his fault that they fought. If only he had never been born. All he remembered of his father was that he never ever listened to him. After Mommy left, he would leave the little six-year-old Aidan at home alone while he went to work and while he drank and carried on with different women; the boy hardly ever went to school. Finally, one of the neighbors who felt sorry for the little boy called the school and made a report, saying she was a concerned neighbor but didn't want to be involved. The school, in turn, called Child Protective Services (CPS). When CPS went out to investigate, they knocked and little Aiden opened the door without hesitation, his dad was nowhere around. Aidan was barefoot, with dirty pajamas on and face plastered with peanut butter. In the kitchen was a mess and stunk of urine, dirty dishes and garbage, and there they also saw a peanut butter jar, with a spoon on the floor that a small dog was now licking. Poor little baby, the social worker thought. Aidan was taken away. His father did show up for court but he looked as if he had slept in his clothes and he reeked of alcohol. Paul had said that he didn't have a job and he had been evicted from the apartment. "You can have him if you want him," he said callously. Of course, after that, there was no question that Aidan would now be a ward of the state. The place he was sent to was the pits but at least he had clean clothes; the food was slop but he ate it and was never hungry anymore like he had been with his dad.

The spirits that followed Aidan were old anger, bullying, and abuse. Victoria also felt that stealing and fighting were with them and you best believe that old man **Fear** was standing with them over in the old demon corner. "Oh Father in heaven, have mercy", she silently prayed as she entered the room. I can do all things, through Christ, Father I need Your strength."

"Good afternoon, Aidan", she sang out cheerfully. He didn't look at her but he did mumble, "I don't see why it's so good." "Hmmm" she replied, "Well it is very good for me!" "Why," Aidan challenged. "Well for starters, I'm alive and breathing; and, because God has had mercy on me to see another day." "Whatever," he spat out. Then Victoria told him that if he didn't want to be here he didn't have to, however, "Since you came of your own free will, 'here's an idea', why don't we try to make the best of this hour." "Shall we?" She added. Again he mumbled, "Whatever." This time she ignored it and instead she asked him why he had said in his original interview that he needed to talk to "God". "Because I do," he said. "Okay Aidan, that part is obvious to me, but what do you want to talk to Him about?," Victoria answered. He said, "Nobody else cares, so why should you?" Victoria spoke softly and calmly, "Aidan, believe it or not, this is not just a job for me. If I didn't care, I wouldn't be here." She told him that she wanted to listen to everything he wanted to say, and if possible, "I would like to help you sort through the things that make you angry." He began to speak first in an angry voice, but the angry voice was eventually turned into a type of sorrow. He told her that he wanted to ask God why He had made him; there had to be a reason. "And I figured He must know why because I sure don't." He said that it didn't make sense to him that God would make somebody 'a great big mistake' like him for no good reason. "So what the heck is the reason?" he said in a harder, louder voice.

"Well first of all, young man, you need to know that God doesn't make mistakes, there is a reason He made you, and there is only one way to find out what the reason is." Victoria then told him, "You need to get to know Him and then you can ask Him yourself." Aidan smirked and said, "Ha ha, very funny." Everyone knows that "God" doesn't talk to people anymore, like He did in the olden days." Victoria smiled and quietly answered, "He talks to me every day." At that Aidan laughed out loud and said, "Lady, I think you need counseling more than me." Victoria didn't smile. She just looked at the boy with a sadness deep in her heart. "Aidan, you wanna know something?" "I can teach you to listen for and hear God's voice **more**." Then he sat up and asked her what she meant by more. She told him that she knew that he knew exactly what she meant because she knew that he had heard God telling him not to do all those wrong things he had been doing. Aidan was very quiet for a moment then he asked her how she knew that. "Ah ha" she thought, thanking the Father that she had heard **His** voice. When Victoria came around the desk she held Aidan's hand for a moment and said, "Look, I know that because He told me so." Before she could say another word, the boy burst into tears and was sobbing uncontrollably and she was still holding his hand and saying, "Everything is going to be all right when you learn to obey His voice." 'Aidan, look at me please." He stopped crying and sniffling. He looked up at Victoria, somewhat embarrassed about crying. Victoria spoke softly in a soothing tone, "You have been hearing His voice since you were a very little child." "Am I right?" "Yes ma'am." "Aidan, you don't have to fear that voice, you have to learn to embrace it instead of becoming angry and acting out."

When Aidan finally opened up, a flood came from him about how he knew that his brother Paulie was going to die when his mother had told Paulie and him not to go to the river and Paulie sneaked out to go anyway. He heard the voice saying don't go with him Aidan. It was said that the river had a strong undercurrent which was the reason Paulie had drowned. Even though Paulie was only eight years old at the time, he was a very good swimmer. That day Aidan had told Paulie that he was sleepy and didn't want to go, after all little Aidan was only five years old. Aidan had said, "Paulie, maybe you shouldn't go either, Mommy said…" Paulie just smiled and said, that she wouldn't find out unless he told. His big brother never, ever came back home. After that, Aidan didn't understand why his mommy never hugged him or talked to him anymore after Paulie went away, it was like he was invisible to her and "Daddy never cared anyway. Aidan began to cry again, softly this time. His mother had left them and his dad never had the time to listen to him at all. Peanut butter was all he ever ate, occasionally some jelly was there too.

Aidan told Victoria how he had begun to act out and to get in trouble, time after time. He told her how things had gone from bad to worse in that place before he went to the foster parents and how he really didn't steal from that kid, and that he just wanted to listen to 'his stupid iPod, he was going to give it back. "That boy accused me of being a thief, and that's why I beat him up!" He then lowered his voice and said, "After that, I could still hear "The Voice" but I didn't want to listen to Him anymore, and I can't hear Him as much now." "I know I need to talk to Him, I just don't know what to say." There was old man **Fear** lurking in the unseen corner again.

Victoria explained to Aidan that God wasn't angry with him and that He hadn't left him, she told him that the Father was waiting for him to surrender all that pain and anger he had inside and let Him in again. "Listen to Him Aidan, you don't need to be afraid. He loves you." Victoria realized now that Aidan wasn't hard at all, it was just the wall he had built to protect himself from the hurt and feelings of rejection that had all but consumed him, causing him to block out "The Voice".

"Come to Me all you who are weary and heavy laden, and I will give you rest" Matthew 11:28.

Victoria said, "Aidan, I want you to memorize and think about this passage; when you return, we'll discuss it." 'Okay?' "Okay, I will he said" then he looked at her; in his eyes she still saw hurt, fear and pain. As he was leaving, he turned and said, "I don't feel afraid or angry right now… thank you." With that she looked around in her mind and spied the peace angel perched above the window. She didn't sense old man **Fear** anymore, but she wasn't taking any chances with that sly old thief. She would continue to pray for Aidan, binding those foul spirits and losing the peace of God over him.

Victoria had her notes for prayer for each person and next to Aidan's notes she drew a sad face and then a smiling face. ☹☺ She knew she would have Victory and that Aidan would also, but what she also knew was that she truly was going to need confidence in Christ's strength working through her. This boy had been abused in the worst way; she knew without even asking that those ugly spirits were harassing him, telling Aidan that nobody wanted him and that he was a BIG mistake. Victoria would continue to pray to Abba Father for help, and to help the Victory to come to all of her new children.

"Now this is the confidence that we have in Him, that if we ask anything according to His will, He hears us. And if we know that He hears us, whatever we ask, we know that we have the petitions that we have asked of Him"
1 John 5:14-15.

Chapter 8 – Time: moving forward

Victoria
The weekend came again at last

That first day was not an easy trek; however, the rest of the week went by somewhat more smoothly. Victoria knew that this was due to her prayers and the prayers of the church intercessors. She had gone to intercessory prayer twice that week crying out and letting the prayer leader know that she needed a fresh new strength for the journey she was on. She had visited with fifteen more young people, she sat and listened to twenty in all. With these young people (rework the first part of this sentence to read smoother) came more anger, lust, hurt, addictions and most of all "**FEAR**". Oh, if only she could just wring his ugly awful neck for what he had done to these children. "You are defeated," she said out loud. Victoria made notes on each one of the files, crying and asking the Holy Spirit to help her to write individual game plans for them. It was 11:30, Friday night but "before I sleep, she said, 'I have to do one more thing." One by one she picked up the files and prayed and cried out to the Most High Father for answers. "What are You going to do for them, Father, how are You going to use me, Lord?" "In myself, I'm just Victoria, Victor Graham's daughter, but I know, "Abba Father" that only in You can I be Victorious, more than a conqueror." "I will trust in You always." She began praying for her family, the government, peace for Jerusalem and all that she could think of to pray about … Victoria fell asleep.

That night she dreamed of the young people she had counseled and there were many others there as well; they appeared to range in age from twelve to about thirty. They were sitting on the ground of a type of desert and they had empty cups that looked dusty and dry as if no liquid had ever been in them. She had a pitcher of liquid in her hands and as she walked among them, she saw pleading eyes. It was as if she could see through to their very souls. They had dried up because of abuse and lack of love and communication. Abuse had stolen away their hopes and dreams, the lives of their very souls seemed to have been snatched away and sucked dry by giant leaches, leaches of poverty, abuse, death and hopelessness. The young people were slumped over, seemingly dead. At that moment the Holy Spirit came upon her reminding her of Ezekiel's account in **chapter 37:3-5**, "The valley of dry bones." **"And He said to me, *'son of man, can these dry bones live?'*** So I answered, *'O Father, You know.'* Again He said to me, *'Prophesy to these bones and say to them, O dry bones, hear the word of the Most High!'* Thus says the Holy One to these bones, *'Surely I will cause breath to enter into you, and you shall live, I will put sinews on you and bring flesh upon you, cover you with skin and put breath in you, and you shall live.' Then you shall know that I AM the Most High God.'"** At this point in her dream, Victoria began to speak what the Father had told Ezekiel to prophesy, pouring liquid from her pitcher into the cups of these young parched lives and they began to sit up. But they were not drinking the cool liquid, it was as if they had no idea what it was for, then she remembered verses 9 and 10, **"Also He said to me, *'Prophesy to the breath, prophesy son of man, and say to the breath, Thus says the Most High: Come from the four winds, O breath and breathe on these slain that they may live.'* So I prophesied as He**

commanded me, and breath came into them, and they lived, and stood upon their feet as an exceeding great army." As she continued walking and talking to these dry lives, that now began to be revived, she would prophesy, reaching down and lifting their hand and cup to their mouths compelling them to drink. As they drank they stood to their feet but not every one of them would drink or stand and Victoria was saddened by the revelation that she wouldn't be able reach all of them, but happy that many of them drank and stood.

When she awakened and saw that it was 5:00am, she grabbed her Bible and journal, as she flipped through pages, looking up Ezekiel's account in her Bible. She began to write everything that she had heard and seen in her dream, and everything the Spirit was ministering to her heart. Wow, Victoria thought out loud, 'So that's it.' "Those evil spirits are lurking around these children trying to keep them oppressed and depressed. Those imps are so afraid of these young people and afraid of what a powerful army they will be for the Most High. When the enemy's lies are exposed to them and these young people find out who they truly are in Christ, the Anointed One, they will wage war on these thieving attackers." FEAR was a big bully but he will have to shrink and disappear so these children can fulfill their destinies. "Father my Savior, I really need You to take over. I need to have less of me and more of You. I need to stop leaning so much on my book understanding from college and concentrate more on the instructions I learned in Bible school, and in my own life experiences with You, and mostly what is in the 'Book of Life.' Father Great and Mighty! "What an amazing encounter!" Victoria went into a praise of dancing and singing, worshipping and thanking God in advance for the answers to every question, until exhausted she lay still and quiet on the floor of her bedroom, waiting to hear instructions for her day. When she arose again she was thinking to herself. "Why is it that the older folks aren't doing more to help the youth?" They seem to have forgotten what it was like to be young. Then she heard the Spirit within her whisper, **Luke 10:2 says "The harvest is plentiful but the laborers are few"**. This reminded Victoria of a paper she had written while in Bible school, "Choosing to be the chosen." As she reflected on her paper, she recalled in her writings that she had stressed that even though we are chosen, we must in turn, choose to accept and carry out our callings. She began to weep with humble gratitude for being chosen for the assignment, and asking "Father, help me to continue to be obedient to Your call."

Victoria and Stephanie
Five Weeks Later

Victoria was five weeks into her sessions with the young people and she had been prophesying to all of their dry places as the Father lead her. For some reason Stephanie Davis was always heavy in Victoria's inner spirit. She continued to pray everything she could for the girl and she mostly prayed in the Spirit throughout the weeks. The verses from Ezekiel continued to play out to Victoria again and again… **"and He said to me, 'son of man, can these dry bones live?' So I answered, 'O Most High, You know'"** Victoria smiled as she remembered this passage from Ezekiel in the valley of dry bones. She clapped her hands and shouted, "YES THEY CAN LIVE, Abba!" Father God, I thank You once again for this great assignment that You have entrusted to me. I know that I am the most unlikely person that people would've expected to get through to these young people, but O my Faithful Father, you know how to take an ordinary person and use them to do extraordinary things. I remember your servant and my old friend Carol, said once that the caterpillar was born to fly, but until he spread his wings he didn't know it. Thank You Father for making Ordinary Victoria Margarete Graham- Hutchinson into "Extraordinary soul winner for Your Kingdom." I am now spreading my spiritual wings to fulfill Your plan and my dream, dear Father, I will win the young people to You through Christ the Anointed One. I will never crawl again, like the "useless" caterpillar that I thought I was, but I will fly like a butterfly, soar like an eagle, and the young ones will soar with me; And to You, O Most High my Elohim, be all glory, forever more. Amen!

"What a wonderful weekend this is going to be," Victoria thought out loud. Again, Stephanie Davis came into her Spirit pushing away all of her thoughts, and she prayed; she didn't like this feeling of dread. Last night she had also had a low feeling inside of her and she was compelled to intercede for Stephanie. Now she was wondering what on earth was going on with this young lady. She had a sinking suspicion when she thought of the man who had picked her up each time she came to counseling and his harsh treatment of her when she left. Every time Stephanie had come to a session in the last five weeks, Victoria was concerned about how much bigger ole man **Fear** had become. Stephanie was nervous and fidgety each time she arrived. During her sessions she would calm down and **Fear** would shrink but toward the end of the session, she would become nervous and **Fear** again would be in Victoria's spiritual eye and growing larger. Victoria would frown and glare at the thought of old man **Fear** and say the name **"Jesus Christ"** just so she could feel him shrink, cower and tremble. She hated how he was ruling this young lady through that man. Of all twenty of the young people, Stephanie was the one that came to Victoria's spirit the most during her quiet time. Then Victoria would think of some of the visible bruises on Stephanie's wrists and arms from time to time. One time in the earlier weeks, she asked what had happened, of course, Stephanie made an excuse and was defensive. Victoria didn't ask again.

She went about getting ready to go run errands but the concern for Stephanie lingered. Victoria continued to pray for her and all of her twenty new children. She then called their names out loud. **Gloria Santiago, Stephanie Davis, Vincent Incorvia, Caleb Austin, Aidan O'Connor, Maurice Rowlands, Tamera Johnson, Linda Wright, Arthur Torrin, Brenda Jacobs, Billy Johnson, Heleana Rodriguez, Jo-Lynne Peyton, Morgan Tipton, Hannah Foster, Ernesto August, Jacob Quarrels, Matthew Johnson, Robert Long,** and little thirteen-year-old **Madison Cambridge.** Tough bunch at first but progress was made as she prophesied to their "dry bones."

Gloria
Saturday

"No necesito este estúpido trabajo de todos modos!" **(I don't want this stupid job anyway)** Gloria yelled back to her boss. "I quit, I'm so tired of you complaining about everything I do. Así que ahora usted puede hacerlo usted mismo!" **(so now you can do it yourself)** "Arrastramiento de grasa **(fat creep!)**," she yelled, storming out of the restaurant and kicking the door as she went out. Gloria continued down the street, cussing to herself in Spanish and in English. She just wished everyone would stop yelling at her and making her angry.

Gloria had worked for this greasy spoon restaurant for almost a year and a half and it was always one thing after another. If the boss wasn't yelling at her, some drunk customer was harrassing her. On top of it all, her sleazy manager was always hitting on her, and in this place there was no such thing as sexual harrassment. Well, Gloria had had it! But now what? She had no money and was already two weeks late with rent for her broken down apartment. "If only the mice and roaches could pitch in, after all they had taken up residence long before she'd moved in." 'Please **HELP** me 'GOD',' she mindlessly said out loud. At that very moment Victoria walked out of the drug store on the corner. Gloria would have run right into her had Victoria not said, "Well good morning, Gloria." At first Gloria jumped trying to recognize her. She was in a sweatsuit with her hair pulled back in a ponytail and no lipstick or any eyeliner. When it came to her who Victoria was, she said, "Lady you look real different, I almost didn't know who the (um er um), heck you were. Victoria smiled and said, "Well I have to be comfortable too sometimes." "Where are you headed?", she added. Gloria said she wasn't headed anywhere and she had just quit her job and now it was starting to rain. After a few more words, Victoria said, "Let's go over here and pray for a minute." After they held hands and Victoria prayed, Gloria asked why it was that she always seemed so happy and why she was so nice to her after the way she acted up that first time they'd met.

Victoria studied the girl for a minute as she whispered, "God help me to help this pretty, but angry young woman." She then told Gloria about the joy of the Father and the love He had placed in her and how she could have it too. Gloria said, "You keep telling me that, and I might just start believing you. Only you just don't know all my problems, lady. "God" don't have time for all the stuff I got going on." Victoria told her that **God IS** time and He has plenty of it. "Gloria listen to me, when we take the time to know Him, He will show us how very much He cares about all of our stuff." After a few more minutes of encouragement Victoria said, I have to go now but let's continue this at our session this week. "Oh and please try to be on time, ok." Gloria frowned and said, "Oh yeah, okay, I'll try." "Umm hmm", Victoria thought. This child had been late every week.

Stephanie
Saturday – the same week
It was pouring down and raining, so why was Stephanie standing in the corner drug store in dark sunglasses and a big sun hat? Walking down the makeup aisle Stephanie grabbed her side as the pain ripped through her, reminding her . . . She ached all over from the beating Rick had given her last night, now here she was looking for make up to cover her black eye. She went back over what had happened the previous night. Rick was always beating up on her for one reason or another but this was the worst one yet. He had never hit her in the face before, but this time he was crazy with rage. One of the customers at the club had lingered around talking to her "too long," Rick had said. She answered, "But I'm a dancer it's my job to entertain the customers." That statement had triggered an anger she had not seen before. He had punched her right in the face, the blow knocked her down to the floor and he had stomped and kicked her until the knock came at the door. The neighbors in the apartments around her had called the police and said someone was being killed. Stephanie had screamed and cried so loudly, that they thought he would kill her this time.

When the police arrived and said, "police, open up", Rick ran out the back door and down the stairs. When Stephanie finally crawled toward the door, they were already inside. They had kicked in the door after they had heard the screaming. She stood but then she collasped into the arms of the female police officer in front of her. The other officer had run through the apartment but Rick was long gone. The young officer called for an ambulance because Stephanie was bleeding from the mouth. She had blacked out.

Stephanie awoke in the ER; realizing where she was and remembering some of her ordeal, she sat up and began getting up from the bed as the police officer was writing the report. He was asking the name of her assailant and a description so he could be arrested and she could press charges as soon as they could pick him up. She was shaking and saying, "No I'm not staying here, you don't understand. I can't press charges and I have to go." The doctor was adamant that she stay overnight for observation, he said that he feared that she could have internal injuries but Stephanie refused, she was so afraid of Rick. With tears welling up, she just said, "I've had internal injuries all my life and I'm leaving now." So please move out of my way. He told her she had to sign a release that she was refusing she was refusing treatment. She scribbled her name on the paper and turned to go, grimacing with each step as she left the hospital. She didn't want to go home to Rick. She was so afraid, but where could she go? The female police officer had noticed Stephanie's purse on the table at her apartment and had brought it to the hospital for identification in case the girl didn't wake up she had said. Luckily for Stephanie she still had all of her tips from the night before. Rick hadn't had time to take most of her money like he usually did. She caught a cab and went to a motel far out by the airport where she knew Rick wouldn't find her. Pain shot through her head pulling her from her reverie. She picked up the concealer and foundation then she went to the pain medicine aisle and got extra strength medication to take for the pain. She paid and as soon as she left the store she opened the pills and chewed four of them. She knew they would work faster if she chewed them. As she headed back to the hotel, she whispered, "God if You're listening, please help me. I don't know what to do anymore and I don't have much more money for this hotel." As she turned the key to go back into her room, her cell phone rang, scaring her. She dropped her purse and as she bent down to pick it up, she cried out from all the pain she was suffering from. She was picking up her belongings and ignoring the phone showing a number she didn't recognize, when she also saw a business card among her things. As she picked it up, the name on the card seemed to jump out at her: "Victoria Hutchinson, Christian Counselor" the number on her phone looked somewhat similar to the number on the card. As she looked at her missed calls the number was the same. "What could she be calling for and why would she be at work on a Saturday?" Stephanie thought out loud.

Chapter 9 – Grace: Salvation is on the way

After Victoria had talked and prayed with Gloria, she was sitting in her car and her phone rang. It was one of the nurses from the hospital, Stacie Chambers, who was also a member of her church and the intercessory team. Stacie had recognized the name on the card that was sticking out of Stephanie's purse the night before. She had thought to herself what a horrible sight this young lady had been in the ER last night, black eyes, big knots on her head, swollen jaw, and bruises everywhere. As she prayed for her, she thought, "Whatever monster did this should be locked up now!" As she looked at the card she thought that this must be one of the young people Victoria Hutchinson was counseling and decided she would call her first thing in the morning.

Victoria answered as she looked at the caller ID. She sang out cheerfully Good morning Stacie. Hi Victoria, she answered, in an urgent-sounding voice. Immediately Victoria knew that this was not a social call, "What is it Stacie?" she said, heart now beating a bit faster. Stacie asked, "Do you know a Stephanie Davis, maybe from your new young clients?" Victoria's heart dropped to her belly as she said, "Yes, I do and she is one of them." Victoria had awakened last night with a strong unction to intercede on behalf of Stephanie. Stacie then began to tell Victoria that she had seen Stephanie in the ER and that she was in big trouble, she said, "If you have her number, you should call her." "Oh Father thank you," she whispered. At least the girl is alive. Hearing that Stacie said, "Yes barely, Victoria, she refused treatment and the doctor was very concerned about maybe some internal bleeding." Victoria asked what had happened. Stacie told her that she had said enough already, all she would say is the child is in bad shape and could use a friend, sooner rather than later. Victoria went straight home to her files to get the number for Stephanie, "Lord have mercy", she prayed as she punched in the numbers. She had used her work cell phone which was always church protocol in the case of a client. Victoria's heart dropped again when she got no answer. She had thought about Stephanie and how that man had grabbed her so roughly as she had watched from her window those days when Stephanie was leaving her office. She remembered the brutish way he handled her and the look of fear on her face and that yellow-toothed creepy grin from old man **Fear**, as Victoria imagined him climbing into the back seat of the car. Victoria remembered the chill that went up the back of her neck and how that chill had lingered as she watched them drive off.

Her work cell phone rang pulling her from her thoughts; it was Stephanie. Victoria answered trying not to sound too concerned yet she had to be somewhat concerned in order to explain her first call. Stephanie said "Hello, is this Ms. Victoria?" "Yes Stephanie, this is Victoria Hutchinson, I called you before because you were on my mind last night and I felt I needed to pray for you." "Is everything alright?" At that moment Stephanie remembered that she had asked 'God' for help, "Could this be His answer?" She immediately dismissed the thought because she knew He couldn't possibly listen to her after all the bad things she had done. The long silence was disturbing to Victoria so she said, "Ok, Stephanie where are you and what is going on?" Stephanie began sobbing, almost uncontrollably. "Stephanie, where are you?" Victoria asked again this time in a more demanding voice, "Are you safe?" Stephanie told her that she was safe but that she wasn't ok, then told her where she was. I'm on my way, don't leave!" Victoria said in an authoritative voice. Stephanie told her she wouldn't leave, that she had used her last money to pay for another night at the motel. Hanging up the phone, Victoria raced toward the airport expressway, thanking God for all the green lights as she went.

Chapter 10 – Victory

Aidan dug the Bible out from under his few clothes and his one pair of sneakers.

Aidan
He was busy brushing his teeth and thinking about the verse Miss Victoria had given him to memorize, **"Come unto Me all you who are weary and heavy laden, and I will give you rest.** Aidan had a strange feeling in the pit of his stomach when he heard, "I have work for you to do son." He looked around and realized that the words came in a quiet kind gentle voice that he thought was in his head. (It came from within him, the Holy Spirit was ministering to him). He tried to shake the thought that He was hearing God. After all, why would the Most High talk to him after everything he had done, and how he had ignored His voice for so long? 'But wait', he thought to himself, I prayed last night to hear Him again.' "Could He be answering me already?" "God, is that You?" Continuing to brush his teeth, again he heard the voice; still, kind and gentle. I am always with you son… always. Aidan knew for sure now that He heard the Most High again. He knew that voice he had heard since he was a little boy.

"Dear God, I don't really know how to pray right so I'm doing my best. I know You can hear me and I'm sure glad I can hear You again. I gotta ask You something. Some people say we shouldn't question You, but I don't know anyone who can answer this question except You. I don't mean any disrespect but, I just feel like this one question will be all right. If You don't answer me then I guess I just gotta try and find out on my own.

God, why did You make me? What am I here for? My Momma said I was her second biggest mistake, but Miss Victoria told me that You don't make mistakes. So I just want to know… if Miss Victoria is right and if I'm not a mistake, then why did You make me? That's all I want to know. I hope You don't take a real long time to tell me Sir, but I'm waiting…. Amen."

What Aidan didn't know was that God hears all prayer but some of the most important prayers are sincere heartfelt prayers, prayed in faith. Because Aidan never received love from his earthly father, he didn't know that the Most High could be a loving and understanding Father and that He really doesn't mind us asking sincere questions. He is, after all, our heavenly Father and if we can't ask Him, who can we ask? He's the only one who can tell us the plan He has for us. Aidan thought to himself and after a long moment said to himself, "Well since I prayed, I guess I better read my Bible." The people at the boys' home had given him one and he kept it in his things wherever he went, but he never really read it. Aidan dug the Bible out from under his few clothes and his one pair of sneakers. After he looked at it a while, he realized that he had no idea where to start; he decided he would just open it and wherever it opened to he would read. When he opened the Bible, he saw **Jeremiah 29**. Aidan began to read, as he read on he saw **verses 11 thru 14**: *"For I know the plans I have for you,"* declares the LORD, *"plans to prosper you and not to harm you, plans to give you hope and a future. Then you will call on me and come and pray to me, and I will listen to you. You will seek me and find me when you seek me with all your heart. I will be found by you,"* declares the Most High, *"and will bring you back from captivity. I will gather you from all the nations and places where I have banished* *you,*" declares the Most High, "*and will bring you back to the place from which I carried you into exile.*" Aidan felt almost like he couldn't breathe, he read it again and again and again until, at last, he understood what Miss Victoria meant when she said that God does still talk to people. "Wow", he said, out loud, "Sir, You really do speak to us and answer our questions and now I know how You do it! You speak though other people like Miss Victoria and You speak through this book. I guess You got a whole lot of other ways You can talk to us if we just listen, like she said!" Now, Aidan decided he would get on his knees and thank God that He had answered him and thank Him for his life, and for His Son Jesus Christ, and for Miss Victoria and for everything he could think of; it just kept getting longer. Every time he started to get up, he thought of something else that he was thankful for. He felt happy again for the first time in a long time.

Chapter 11 – Conscience

Stephanie was now drifting in and out of consciousness; however, she had been coherent enough to tell them about Rick; Richard Rowlands.

Stephanie
"Father! Have mercy", Victoria said out loud when Stephanie opened the door of the motel room. Even with the shades pulled in the dark little room she could see this young woman and the terrible condition she was in. Nurse Stacie had been right when she said the girl was in trouble and was barely alive. Victoria was immediately praying in both English and in the Spirit. "Stephanie, honey, we need to get you to the hospital A.S.A.P." Stephanie began crying uncontrollably again, "No, I can't, he will find me and he will kill me. He said so, he said, if I get him in trouble, he will kill me." Victoria kept on praying as she called 911 for an ambulance and the police, while mumbling under her breath, 'If we don't get you to the ER he might not have to.' "Now you listen to me young lady, no one is going to get past our God or me, to kill you, and the police will make sure of that too, and this time you are going to give them his information and he will be arrested and prosecuted. He will go to jail, I'll make sure of that." Victoria took out her phone and began taking pictures of all the bumps and bruises. Stephanie was in bad shape and Victoria thought she was on the verge of death. Sirens drew nearer and nearer until they at last stopped outside. Victoria opened the door and light rushed into the dark room; when Stephanie stood to go to the bathroom she collapsed in a heap on the floor; that's when Victoria saw the blood on the bed and on Stephanie. "Oh

Father in heaven, Victoria exclaimed." She prayed in the ambulance all the way to the hospital.

The doctors at the hospital confirmed what the other doctor from the ER last night had believed. Stephanie had internal injuries. They asked Victoria about next of kin, and she thought of Stephanie's file and those rotten step brothers. No way would she even mention them as if they even deserved to be called next of kin. She also remembered that Stephanie's mother was named Mable Ann Davis, but she had no idea where the woman lived. Stephanie was now drifting in and out of consciousness; however, she had been coherent enough to tell them about Rick; Richard Rowlands she had said. He works at the Marcel Gentleman's Club on East 25th Street. She gave them a somewhat accurate description before she lost consciousness again. Doctors now determined she had lost so much blood that she needed a transfusion. They began treatment.

Victoria remembered that when she had looked out the window on those days, that the man she saw drove a late model silver Toyota Avalon, the license plate read Playa-1. She also remembered that he had a tattoo on the side of his neck, of a skull and cross bones, inside of a web with a black spider in it. One of the police officers recognized the man's description from a prior arrest for domestic violence from three years back he would never forget. The case had been dismissed; for some reason the young woman refused to testify. "That one had been roughed up pretty badly, but she had nowhere near the extent of the injuries this young lady has sustained," he stated, shaking his head. Later as they checked more into the Marcel Gentlemen's Club,-they realized that the other young lady who was beaten by Rick had also been a dancer there, but had left town.

Victoria was on the phone to one of the intercessors at church. Charity Livingston was now armed with prayer and on her way to Regional Memorial Medical Center located in Hanover County, within Richmond, Virginia. This had been the closest hospital from Richmond Airport. At the same time, the hospital had located the correct Mable Ann Davis; she too was on her way to the hospital. Mable had left work at the café and as usual, was worried more about her job than she was about Stephanie. The ER doctors were waiting to get permission for surgery to stop the bleeding. Stephanie had lost a tremendous amount of blood and no doubt needed more blood transfusions for which a release needed to be signed. She had signed the first release but was in no shape to give permission for surgery. The ER had been all a buzz as Stephanie lay there unconscious her face swollen, eyes shut but not from unconsciousness, and she was black and blue all over. The poor child was barely recognizable wearing a grayish cast on her face like a shadow of death.

Charity Livingston arrived in warrior mode, she saw Victoria and went to her. As they embraced, she noticed Victoria's tear-streaked flushed face. Victoria then turned her head away from Charity's eyes. "Hurry up Mable Ann Davis," Victoria said out loud. Now she was fidgeting. Charity laid her hand gently upon Victoria's saying into her ear, "Be still my dear, this is in God's hands now, you did your part, so now leave it to Him." Victoria sat down and began praying as Charity joined in. They waited for Mable.

Vincent

This was a hard job and Vincent wasn't feeling it at all. The foreman had refused to call him Vincent when he asked him to, he told him to shut up and do the job. "Vinnie is easier," he added, and that he could call him "hey you" if he wanted to.

Vincent's cousin, Laura, worked in the office at the bread plant and was able to get him the job in spite of his felony conviction. However much he hated the hard work, working Saturdays and the long hours, Vincent knew he needed this job, it paid good wages, and he was determined not to get into any more trouble, so that was incentive enough for him to keep working and to keep his mouth shut. His parole officer had told him that if he blew off this job, he was going back to prison to serve the other four years he had gotten out of serving. "Good behavior, my eye" the parole officer had snorted, "You are as bad as they come, and you won't change either, I'm just waiting for the day I catch you so I can send your P.K. hind parts right back to prison. And I 'will' catch you, you can bank on it," Kenneth Caruthers growled.

Vincent as he now preferred to be called, thought to himself, "You won't catch me ever again because I'm gettin myself together." Believe it or not, Vincent Incorvia had committed his last crime. He had gone to church on Wednesday night with his new friend Howard Jones. All Howard ever talked about was Jesus and how He had saved and changed his life. Vincent had met Howard at the mall one day. Howard was outside the mall passing out Bible tracts. As Vinnie was going to buy a pair of steel-toe boots for his new job, Howard said, "Hey man I got some important news for you." Vincent had thought to himself, "Bible thumper" then he thought again, maybe he should listen.

Something inside of him reminded him of last night when his mom, Celeste, had told him she was praying that someone would get through to him, she'd said things like "Tomorrow is not promised, and you need to repent and surrender to God." Then she quoted scripture that had bugged him half the night. The Holy Spirit says, **"Today if you hear God's voice, harden not your heart" Hebrews 3:7.** He kept hearing the verse over and over. Vincent decided he would listen to Howard today. Howard went on and on about how he was headed straight to hell, how drugs and alcohol had been his only comfort, until he found the Savior, The Anointed One, and "The change is phenomenal," Howard had said to Vincent. Wow this guy was so passionate and so happy Vincent decided right then and there he was going to attend Howard's church. He scribbled his address, handed it to him and Howard said, "I'll pick you up Wednesday evening at 7:00 sharp." As Vincent entered the mall he felt an old sensation of happiness and satisfaction like he had when he was fifteen and teaching Sunday school.

Howard had walked down to the Altar Wednesday night to support Vincent as he rededicated his life to God. Vincent still wasn't totally rid of old Vinnie, but it was a start. He could hardly wait for his session with Victoria. That lady was on the ball when it came to knowing the scriptures and their meanings, it was even better than when she knew the meanings of all of those "V" names she spoke to him about in the beginning session.

Stephanie
Victoria paced the floor of the hospital hallway. It was 2:00pm, they had taken Stephanie into surgery at 11:30. "What on earth was going on in that O.R.?"

The doctors didn't seem too optimistic so Victoria had prayed a prayer of repentance and salvation with Stephanie before they wheeled her into surgery. She and Charity Livingston continued praying, going back and forth to the hospital chapel to escape Stephanie's mother and her whining. Mable Davis sat in a corner by the window; she had complained and fretted so much about how she would lose her job that Victoria abruptly walked away from the woman while Mable was in midsentence. How dare she talk about her petty little job when she didn't know if her child would live or die! "Maybe if you'd paid more attention to Stephanie and less to that job, she wouldn't be in here now fighting for her life," Victoria thought. As true as that might be, Victoria immediately began to feel conviction for that thought and for being so harsh and judgmental, she was worried about Stephanie. Still that was no excuse to misrepresent God. She should be using that energy on drawing the woman to Christ. She repented by I John 1:9 and later returned to where Mable sat and apologized for her rudeness in walking away while she was still talking.

As she sat down, she held Mable's hand and prayed for Stephanie and for restoration of the mother and daughter's relationship with the Almighty and with each other. When she opened her eyes, tears streamed down Mable Davis' face. Victoria continued to hold her hand until they saw the surgeon walking toward them.

Victoria's heart sank at the grim look on the man's face. Mable squeezed her hand so tight it ached, the woman was trembling like a leaf on a tree, in Chicago, in the fall. She looked about ready to pass out when Victoria gently placed her arm around Mable's shoulder and steadied her. "She's a strong young woman," Victoria whispered. After what seemed like an hour the surgeon was standing before the three women. "The surgery was successful, we were able to stop the bleeding, but she is not out of the woods yet. She lost a lot of blood and her injuries were very extensive. The next 24 to 48 hours are crucial, we've done all we can for her, just need to hope and pray now," he said. He then turned to Victoria and said, "If she makes it, it will be because you got her in here in the nick of time, and had she stayed last night the outcome may have been much better." They thanked the surgeon.

Stephanie was taken to ICU and kept under strict observation. Under normal circumstances she would only be allowed two visitors at a time, however, since Minister Charity was clergy, she was allowed to stay. Since she was a widow and had no one at home to answer to Charity opted to stay and continue praying at Stephanie's bedside. Before Victoria knew it Charity Livingston had ministered to Mable and she had said the sinner's prayer. Mable no longer seemed concerned about her job, at least she had stopped fidgeting and talking about it. Charity told Victoria she should go home and rest because she looked exhausted. "If anything happens, I'll call you." Victoria told her to call her the moment Stephanie awakened, she then went to Mable and told her she would be back in a while.

As Victoria pulled into her driveway, she could feel tears burning the backs of her eyelids. She had held it in all day but she could hold it no longer. As soon as she put the car in park she began sobbing out loud, tears streaming down her face. She turned off the engine and cried for fifteen straight minutes and then more off and on until she could compose herself.

She was barely in the door when her cell phone began ringing. She jumped and her heart raced as she fumbled through her purse for it. She looked at the screen and it read Justin Saunders, Victoria composed herself as best she could. 'Hello honey,' she answered.' "Mom, is that you?" Justin asked. "Yes, hi Justin" She tried to sound calm, but Justin knew his mother. "What's going on and why'd it take so long for you to answer?" Victoria now found herself trying to convince her son that she was all right, as he kept threatening to get on a plane. Victoria took a deep breath and sat in the recliner as she began telling her son about the ordeal, without revealing any names. She normally would not have told him but it was the only way she could convince him that she was ok and he didn't need to come to her rescue.

Justin now understood what he had heard in Victoria's voice when she first answered the phone. He remembered that his mother had been in an abusive relationship with his stepdad when he was a boy. He remembered that he had vowed to take care of the creep as soon as he got bigger. However, he didn't have to because his stepdad was killed in a car wreck while he was DUI. He also remembered being happy that he never had to see him again. Those feelings changed when his mom began going to church, and he got involved with the youth group. He actually felt bad then and hoped that his stepfather had had the time to repent; as bad as that man was, Justin didn't like the thought of anyone having to be separated from God, in hell forever. A chill went up his spine at the very thought of it.

Justin had always been a good kid and he embraced the faith immediately. He gave his mom all the credit for his becoming an ordained minister and eventually the youth pastor at his church in Seattle. Victoria had always encouraged him, all of his friends had always liked her; she was like the block "Mama."

Justin had a lovely wife and three beautiful children: one boy and two girls. Victoria had always been a good mother and Justin's dad had died in a boating accident when Justin was in second grade. It had been an emotional and financial struggle for them until Forest Hutchinson came along with his big money and a nice car. Forest had wooed Victoria until she agreed to marry him but within months he became verbally abusive and after a year it became physical.

Justin had been so afraid for his mom but she kept blaming herself for making Forest angry. Justin hated the creep from the beginning but his mom couldn't see the darkness Justin felt when Forrest came around. He didn't kick and scream because she seemed happy again but only for a short time. Forrest Hutchinson had been Justin's three-year nightmare, a series of drunken rages and 911 calls had become the norm. Justin also remembered plotting with his friends how they were going to pay Larry Thompson to beat up Forrest. Larry was a big football player at the high school and he always came to throw the football around with the little kids. They were putting their money together to pay him, but before they could save enough, Larry was going away to college. Justin remembered crying about that since he had no other plan to help his mom.

Well as fate would have it, Forrest was taken out of their lives just as abruptly as he had come in. Justin and Victoria had gone to his funeral but neither of them ever shed a tear. After the funeral they talked about it and Victoria promised Justin that she would never let this kind of thing ever happen to them again. The next man in their lives was Christ, The Anointed One and He was the only one that they both ever needed. Justin and Victoria talked on the phone a bit longer, then said goodnight.

As Victoria sat in the recliner going over the events of the day, she dozed off, not realizing how tired she was she fell into a deep sleep. When she awakened, with a start, she realized that she was at home; she had been dreaming that she was still at the hospital. She got up out of the chair a bit stiff but she picked up her phone to call Charity. She was assured that Stephanie was sleeping peacefully, that Mable was determined to stay until her daughter awakened and that she need not come back until morning. Victoria took out her nightgown and headed in the bathroom for a nice hot shower. She washed her hair and stepped out. After drying off, she decided to read a few chapters in Ecclesiastes before praying. Victoria finally went to sleep and did not awaken until 7:00 am which is late for her. Preparing for church, she decided she would run by the hospital and then go to 11:00 service instead of her usual routine of going to 8:30 service. Apparently, Rick had entered the hospital and the assigned police officer who had arrested him before, knew immediately who he was.

Stephanie
Victoria arrived at the hospital to find the parking area flashing blue with two police cars out at the front door. "Oh my Father, what
now?" She said as she parked. Half running, she was barely inside the door when she saw the officers wrestling with

someone on the floor, at that moment Victoria recognized the skull & crossbones inside the spider in a web on the side of the young man's neck. It was him, that horrible monster who had beaten Stephanie to within an inch of her life. Rick had gone everywhere and called every hospital in the area until he found Stephanie. The officers had him handcuffed and on his feet when she scooted by unnoticed. She thought that he had never actually seen her but she also didn't know if Stephanie had revealed her name or pointed her out anywhere else, but she didn't want to look at him until they were in the courtroom.

Charity and Mable were still in the room hovering over Stephanie like German Shepherds with new puppies. Stephanie's eyes were still closed as Victoria came closer to the bed and she mouthed to the women, "What on earth happened?" Charity had been on her way back up from the cafeteria when the whole thing was taking place. She had run back to the room to be sure Stephanie was ok. Mabel had described the man to Charity during the night and she recognized him immediately. Rick had no idea that Stephanie had talked to anyone, let alone that they had a warrant for his arrest. As he walked to the desk to ask for Stephanie's room number he noticed that the officer, who had already radioed for backup, was walking toward him. As Rick turned to run, the other two officers were coming through the door. As he continued to run, trying to escape, there was a janitor mopping the floor and just as he flung the mop out on the floor Rick tripped over it and down he went. In half of a second, all three officers were on him. Victoria had seen it from that point. "Thank you, Abba" she said lifting her hands.

"Has she been awake at all?" Victoria asked. "Somewhat in and out." Mable answered but she doesn't know he was here. The woman had dark circles under her eyes and looked as if the weight of the world was on her shoulders. Victoria decided right then that she wasn't going to church and told Mable she should go home, Charity chimed in as Mable tried to refuse. After five or ten minutes of these two doubling up on her she finally relented. "Charity, you can go too, you're due for a bit of rest yourself," Victoria said, with a look that said, 'don't try me.' Charity knew that look all too well and although she was several years Victoria's senior, she also knew that her arguing would be futile.

She picked up her purse and said, "Yes ma'am" with a smile and a hug and she followed Mable out. Charity turned to Victoria and said, "I'll be back but if anything changes before I get here, you call me and I mean it." "Ok, now just go, and I'll call you too, Mable." She nodded and smiled weakly as she all but dragged herself out of the door. Stephanie stirred but didn't open her eyes; Victoria, shaking her head sadly, looking at the child's black eye, swollen lip, and multiple bruises, continued silent prayers.

As the two women walked down the corridor to leave the hospital, Charity noticed the sad look on Mable's face. "Try to cheer up Mable, I've been praying and so has Victoria, I believe our heavenly Father is faithful to bring your child back whole." Mable was crying now. She told Charity that she had prayed too but when Stephanie did wake up, she wasn't sure that she would even talk to her. They had said horrible things to each other on their last meeting. Stephanie had also told her what a rotten, uncaring mother she had been, and that she had called her selfish and now she knew that her daughter was right. She had been the most selfish, unconcerned mother ever and she couldn't really blame Steph for saying she never wanted to see her again.

Charity held the woman, trying to console her but her wound was so much deeper than what she had revealed that the sobbing went on for at least 10 minutes. She also told Charity that her boss had called her last night and told her if she wasn't at the restaurant by 8:30 that she was fired. "I just couldn't bear to leave Steph last night especially after never being there for her when she needed me most," Mable sobbed. "There-there, now child, you'll make yourself sick," Charity comforted. "Besides, our Father above is able to heal all those old wounds if we just ask and believe Him." "As far as that job is concerned, it probably was high time you got out of there anyway. God can open another door and give you something way better honey, you just gotta learn to trust Him." "Now dry up them tears and put away them keys, cause you coming home with me," Charity told her.

She took Mable home with her, gave her something to eat and drink, then she showed her to the guest room. "Now, there's a bath in your room through that door (pointing). There are towels and extra toothbrushes in that linen closet; I'll get you a gown and some fresh clothes for later. I think we're bout the same size." "You just go to sleep and I'll wake you when I'm ready to go back." Charity closed the door. Mable showered and got into the gown, she was exhausted, she had been on a double at the restaurant when she got the call. It had been over 48 hours since she had slept. As she uttered "Thank You, Father," she fell asleep before her head could hit the pillow.

Caleb

Caleb told Reverend Tee all about his sessions with Victoria these last five weeks and how she gave him scripture verses to memorize each week. "Afternoon Caleb, I didn't expect to see you again today and on a Sunday afternoon," Reverend Trolli sang out as he entered the double doors of the community center, "What's up?" "I got some questions Rev. Tee" Caleb answered with a most pensive look on his face. Samuel Trolli's curiosity was peaked. He sat down next to the young man and said, "I'm all ears."

The one verse that stuck to him like a fly on a flytrap was the first one she had given him. **"And though your beginning was small your latter days will be great" Job 8:7.** "Rev does that mean what I think it means?" Because the counselor said it does."

Caleb went on to tell Reverend Trolli that he thought it meant the next part of his life was supposed to be great. Miss Victoria said I was right and that I could become great if I would just apply myself and develop a relationship with Almighty God. "Well I been reading my Bible, I been coming here helping out, I been going to church with the Roberts (Miss Rose and Mr. Mike), and I been praying, but God ain't said nothin yet, I don't think He can hear me and I don't know what I'm doing wrong." Caleb sounded so frustrated.

Reverend Tee told him that he wasn't doing anything wrong and that God hears all prayers, but that sometimes people are so busy talking that they can't hear what He is saying. He explained to Caleb that the voice of God is seldom audible to hear with our physical ears. "We have to listen with spiritual ears Caleb, and let me clarify that for you." "God speaks to our spirit on the inside of us in a still small voice." He reminded Caleb of how he had taught him about how we are three parts: spirit, soul and body and how the spirit is where God communicates with us and how the soul is the human part of us in which our physical attributes are housed. "You can't listen with these ears son," Reverend Tee said, as he touched his ears. "We have to listen for Him from within our Spirit man" he then touched his stomach. "Is this making sense son?" "I think so" Caleb still looked confused.

Rev. Tee grabbed Caleb's hands and said, "Lets pray." He prayed for Caleb to receive wisdom and understanding by the Holy Spirit, and that the eyes of his understanding be enlightened. He also asked the Most High to supply these things liberally as the Bible promises. Once he ended the prayer, he told Caleb that the next time he prayed, he wanted him to set aside thirty minutes. "I want you to get in a quiet place by yourself and turn off your cell phone, pray and ask God to help you to hear His voice, but I want you to pray for only five minutes; the other twenty-five minutes I want you to clear your thoughts and just listen."

He gave Caleb a CD of soothing sounds and quiet music, he told him to let this CD help him to relax his mind. "Don't be impatient now, just keep doing this until you hear God's voice down on the inside, then come tell me when you hear it." Caleb looked puzzled, then he said, "You said 'when' I hear it, so you believe He's really gonna talk to me?" "I know He will, if you listen," Rev. Trolli assured him. "Well then, I know He will too

Rev", Caleb smiled.

That night, Caleb went up on the roof of the farm house, boom box in hand. He had plugged it in downstairs and connected it to the long orange extension cord; Caleb sat down. He now lived away from the city on a farm, His new foster parents were nice and the bus ran till 6 pm and stopped a ½ mile down the road. He thought to himself, I know He can hear me up here, this is the quietest place I know." Caleb's foster mother knew that he would go up there to be alone and it was ok, he was quite a bit older than the other two fosters they had there.

Caleb begin his prayer by thanking the Father, like Miss Victoria and Reverend Trolli always emphasized. He then began talking to the Father about how much he wanted to hear His voice. He told Him that His mother had always said that Someone up there 'likes me' and "I really want to hear that Someone." "I want You to help me to know that I'm not a "sorry boy" and that I can be somebody who can make a difference in life. He said Amen and as he listened to the music mingled with crickets and owls. He smiled to himself. "Now I know I'll hear You, Abba." About an hour later, Caleb heard someone call him, the voice was small but urgent. It didn't sound like his foster dad, Mr. Mike, but it had to be him, he was the only man in the house.

Miss Rose was in the kitchen, heating up the dinner. "Where's Mr. Mike, I heard him call me?" Caleb asked. "Well, I don't see how you heard him all the way over here, he's been out in the barn for an hour messing around and cleaning up behind that old horse. I'm heating up his food now, why don't you go get him for me."

Walking Among Dry Bones – Cynthia Atkinson pg. 88

Caleb headed out to the barn thinking he was sure someone had called him, then he felt an incredible urge to hurry so he began jogging. When he opened the barn door, Mr. Mike was laying on the hay floor of the barn, Caleb knew he wasn't sleeping because he was right in the middle of the floor. He ran over to where the man was lying, he put his ear on his chest, his heart was beating but it didn't sound right and he thought Mr. Mike wasn't breathing.

Caleb tore out of the barn and ran across the yard like he had wings on his shoes, he was yelling Miss Rose, Miss Rose, hurry, it's Mr. Mike. Rose couldn't hear what he was yelling but her stomach felt like the bottom dropped out. She turned off the stove and headed to the door. Caleb came inside breathing hard, "Miss Rose, call 911 now!"

He then turned and ran back to the barn. He had just remembered the firemen that had come to the boy's home when he was in there. Caleb ran to Mr. Mike and began doing everything the fireman had shown him. He was thinking, he was so glad that he had paid attention. He heard sirens and Mr. Mike coughing all at the same time. By this time Miss Rose was in the barn saying "Caleb what can I do?" "Go show the ambulance where to come." Caleb answered. Miss Rose was crying but she ran out and was waving her hands at the ambulance.

Upon entering the barn, they could see the young man holding the older man's hand and trying to comfort him. Mr. Mike had been breathing now and said a few words. Caleb told the paramedics everything that happened. They had gotten on the phone with the hospital and had been instructed to start an I.V.

and bring Mr. Michael Roberts to the hospital. "You may have saved his life young man, good job" the one paramedic said to Caleb as they wheeled the gurney carrying Mr. Mike to the ambulance. Miss Rose asked Caleb to keep an eye on the others while she went with her husband. "I got it Miss Rose and I'm praying too, don't you worry, just take care of Mr. Mike and bring him back home." Caleb said. Miss Rose hugged Caleb, thanked him and got into the ambulance.

Caleb got the others into bed after their bath and reassured them that the Taylors would be home soon. He got into the recliner and began praying for Mr. Mike and Miss Rose, they were so nice to him. "Please God, let him be ok and help Miss Rose not to worry so much." "And Sir, I know that it was You who called me, I just know it! Thank you, and please talk to me again soon, but can you say a little more than just my name…. Please" Amen. Caleb fell asleep right there in the chair next to the phone.

Chapter 12 – Awakening

Stephanie

"You're still in the hospital Stephanie, how are you feeling?" Victoria asked, now standing next to the bed. "I feel like I got hit by a ton of bricks.

It was now 3:45 in the evening when Stephanie began to stir and opened her eyes. Victoria was still by her bedside but had dozed off. Stephanie's mouth felt dry and tasted awful and when she turned her head it ached badly but she saw Victoria open her eyes. "Stephanie, you're awake," Victoria sat up smiling. "Where am I?" Stephanie asked, with a confused look. "You're still in the hospital Stephanie, how are you feeling?" Victoria asked, now standing next to the bed. "I feel like I got hit by a ton of bricks. I dreamed I saw my mother here, and she kissed me…." Stephanie's words trailed off as she looked toward the window with tears in her eyes. Where are my kids, are they still at my cousin's house? Victoria told her that it wasn't a dream and that Mable had been here all day yesterday and all night and the kids are fine and still at Jodi's house. "I had to make your mother leave because she looked like she was gonna pass out." Stephanie's eyes had a look of disbelief, but she knew Ms. Victoria wouldn't lie to her, so she said, "are you sure the lady was my mother? What about her job?" Victoria told her that she had sat with Mable and knew that the job meant nothing to her when she had seen her little girl in this place fighting for her life.

"That is so hard to believe. That job always meant everything to her, and they were never even nice to her down there; I never could understand why she stayed." She told Victoria how smart her mother was and she could have gone to school and gotten a better job, but that she never believed she could do it. "Now that sounds real familiar to me, sort of like someone else I know," Victoria said with one hand on her hip.

Just then the doctor walked in with two nurses. "Well, look who is finally awake," the doctor belted out, so loud Stephanie's ears rang. "Could you tone it down a little doc, I got some type of serious headache."

They began poking and prodding, so Victoria excused herself from the room. She immediately called Mable's number. No answer. She hung up and called Charity. It had been 2:40 when she and Mable had left four hours earlier. Charity answered and Victoria told her that Stephanie was awake but that the doctor was in with her, so she wasn't sure what was what. She said she needed to find Mable in case the doctor needed to speak with family. "I'm getting no answer on her cell," Victoria told Charity. "Oh, she's right here with me, her phone is in the other room." Charity answered. "We were just about to head over there." "Oh good then I'll see you both shortly." They hung up.

The doctor told Victoria they needed to take Stephanie up for X-rays and that he was ordering an MRI since the headache was so intense and she wasn't feeling her legs below the thigh. "What a nightmare Victoria thought. By the time Charity and Mable arrived Stephanie had been taken to X-ray. It was now 4:30 on Sunday evening and Victoria hadn't prepared anything for the week ahead, she would have to rely totally on Holy Spirit to help her wing it. And who else better to get the job done?

They brought Stephanie back up at 5:20. Charity had promised that she would stay with Mable and Stephanie to serve as a type of mediator. Mable was anxious and fidgety just like Stephanie. Victoria imagined old man **FEAR** was happy about that.

She drove home thinking of a nice hot bubble bath.

Stephanie was a bit cool but cordial to her mother at first, while poor Mable struggled to make conversation with her once estranged daughter. Charity kept the mood light as best she could when all of a sudden, Stephanie finally blurted out what she was wondering the whole time. "Why aren't you at work, did they close down or something?" "Can't figure any other way you got out of being there, you never could get off for me any other time."

Mable just stood there speechless, so Charity felt the need to try to soothe the harshness of Stephanie's verbal attack on her mother. "Now Stephanie," Charity chided, "Your mother has been here day and night for you, She was fired from her job because she felt you were more important." Stephanie swallowed hard and asked, "Who are you?" "Oh never mind." "It doesn't matter, now that I'm an adult and can take care of myself!" This time Mable chided, "It looks to me as if you're not doing a very good job of it, and I know that's partly my fault for not hearing you or teaching you how to do that." "For that Stephanie LaTrese Davis, I do apologize, I can't change what's happened in the past but if you would please give me a chance, I'll try my best to do a better job now."

Stephanie felt ashamed at having been so vicious toward her mother, but it had been the truth. After a long silence, she said, I'm sorry Momma, I'm just tired and I hurt everywhere. Mable picked up the call nurse bell and pushed the button, "Can I help you?" came the voice on the intercom. "Yes, my daughter needs something for pain." "Coming" was the reply. The nurse came in; she used one syringe to put something into the I.V. and the other one she shot into Stephanie's backside. "That should keep her comfortable for a few hours ma'am" "Thank you" Mable returned. When the nurse left the room, Stephanie was already headed to la-la land but she thanked her mother before she was all the way out. Mable was crying again and Charity comforted her and prayed with her.

At home again Victoria had looked over her schedule for the week, shifting things around due to the fact that Stephanie wouldn't make it to her appointments. She ran her bath and stepped in. Once out of the bath she turned on the kettle for a nice cup of lavender rose tea. She prepared her tea, got out her Bible, put on soft instrumental worship music and headed for the recliner for some much-needed R & R.

Chapter 13 – Calling out

Gloria
Monday at 10:00am

"Yes Gloria and He hears you too. Now it's time for you to start listening to Him. He is working on your behalf, so you could spend a little more time with Him listening and not so much talking. I want you to memorize and think about this verse this week.

It was 10:12 and Gloria was not there yet. "What is it with this girl that she can never be on time?" Victoria thought, drumming her fingers on the desk. Just as she started to stand, in ran Gloria. "Necesita agua," Gloria stated. "What on earth happened to you Gloria?" Victoria stood and got a bottle of water from the small refirgerator and handed it to Gloria. Sorry I'm late Miss Victoria but this time it wasn't my fault. I was so proud I was going to finally be on time when the bus hit the car in front of him four blocks from here. I got off the bus and ran here." "For real ma'am I ain't lyin, you can look at the news there was TV cameras and everything." "Ok Gloria, I really need to get started because I have somewhere to go this morning.

"Well guess what, Miss V, oops I mean Miss Victoria" 'What?' "I went to church again yesterday, that's two Sundays and Wednesday night." Gloria proudly stated. Victoria told her that was nice and asked her what she had learned. Gloria rambled on and on about what was said but never really said she had learned anything.

"Gloria please listen to me ok," Victoria stated as gently as she knew how. She knew what a powder keg Gloria could be when offended. Gloria said ok sure. Victoria began to explain that while it was nice that she was going to church and hearing what they were saying, it was equally important that she apply the principles. She told her the importance of having her own relationship with God and studying her Bible on her own to know it for herself. Some of what Victoria was hearing from Gloria was not biblically acurate and she wasn't sure if Gloria had heard it right or just interpreted it differently. Victoria asked Gloria how the rest of her Saturday had gone after she quit her job. "Oh snap. Yeah they called me asking me to come back. I told them I needed a raise and some more respect." Gloria had also asked to have some Saturdays and more Sundays off sometimes. They had agreed to the raise, promised more respect and some weekends off. "Miss Victoria, that prayer you prayed was bangin', it worked. God just be hearin' you."

"Yes Gloria and He hears you too. Now it's time for you to start listening to Him. He is working on your behalf, so you could spend a Little more time with Him listening and not so much talking. I want you to memorize and think about this verse this week. **"Call to Me, and I will answer you, and show you great and mighty things, which you do not know" Jeremiah 33:3.**

Victoria finished her session with Gloria by giving her more to read but not from the Bible. She gave her a book that was written by a twenty-one-year-old girl, who told of her relationship with the Most High and how He had changed things for her after both her parents had been killed in a wreck because of a drunk driver. Since the book wasn't long she asked her to read the first half and be prepared to discuss it next session. They prayed and Gloria left.

Victoria had a mammogram today at 11:30 so her next appointment with Aidan wasn't until 3:00. Her last appointment was Caleb at 4:00, then she was done for the day. She was glad she had scheduled a short day today. She had scheduled her appointment with Stephanie for Wednesday at the hospital, so she wouldn't be going back there until then. She kept up only through Charity, she wanted to get her relationship with Stephanie back to being more professional, but still as personable as she was with everyone else.

Aidan
Monday at 3:00pm
Aidan was so anxious to tell Miss Victoria about his experience last weekend, he felt as if he would jump out of his skin. Victoria was just returning from her mammogram and a late lunch.

"Well, good afternoon Aidan," Victoria sang out, entering her office, as cheerfully as she could, "How are you today," she added. "I'm great Miss Victoria, I really am." Aidan stood by the window, face beaming because he couldn't sit down right now. The excitement was more than he could take, he took a deep breath before he blurted out, "He's talking to me again, Miss Victoria, really talking," he said smiling, "and I heard Him more than once." He now walked over and sat in the chair across from her.

"This is such great news, Aidan and I really need some good news right now," Victoria smiled as she said it. Aidan wasn't buying the smile, after all he had picked up a little discernment of his own while building his newfound relationship with the Most High. "Miss Victoria, I don't mean anything negative but you look tired and not as happy as usual," Aidan said with a look of genuine concern. Victoria dismissed it with a wave of the hand. "Oh it's nothing to concern yourself with, son. "Apparently you've had quite an exciting weekend and I want to hear all about it so let's hear it." She spoke intently as not to give him opportunity to question her further.
Aidan began to relive his weekend. Telling Victoria of his encounters with God.

He told her how God had begun speaking to him, "On Saturday morning, while I was busy, brushing my teeth, I was thinking about the first verse you gave me to memorize, **"Come unto Me all you who are weary and heavy laden, and I will give you rest."** "I had a strange feeling in the pit of my stomach as I heard someone speaking, I asked 'Is that You God? Then I heard this,' "I have work for you to do son." I was looking all around like, it felt like someone was in the bathroom with me, then I realized that the words came in a small gentle voice and I thought it was in my head, but it had come from somewhere closer, within me, you know. I was thinking it was that Holy Spirit you're always telling me about."

"At first, I tried to shake the thought that I was hearing God, and then I got to thinking, why would the Most High talk to me again after all the bad stuff I had done, and how I had kept on ignoring His voice for so long? But then I thought again about how I had prayed the night before, to hear His voice again." So now I was asking myself, could He be answering me already?" "So I said, "God, is that You?"

I kept brushing my teeth, and then I heard Him again!" "I heard the voice, Miss Victoria still, small and gentle just like you said. He said, "I am always with you son… always. Then I knew for sure now that I heard the Most High again. He was really talking to me." Aidan told Victoria how he had prayed some more after that and "Then I thought that since I prayed, I guess I better read my Bible that the people at the boys' home had given me." I had to dig it out from under my clothes and sneakers." He told Victoria that after he realized he had no idea where to start; he decided he would just open it and wherever it opened to he would read. "When I opened the Bible, Miss Victoria, it landed right on Jeremiah 29, and I read it but when I saw verses 11 thru 14, I understood." "***For I know the plans I have for you,***" declares the LORD, "***plans to prosper you and not to harm you, plans to give you hope and a future. Then you will call on me and come and pray to me, and I will listen to you. You will seek me and find me when you seek me with all your heart. I will be found by you,***" declares the Most High, "***and will bring you back from captivity. I will gather you from all the nations and places where I have banished you,***" declares the Most High, "***and will bring you back to the place from which I carried you into exile.***"

Aidan told Victoria that, at first, he felt like he could hardly breathe, but then once he regained composure, he read it again and again and again. "I understand, Miss Victoria," Aidan said with tears in his eyes. You meant that God does still talk to people and answers our questions. "Now I know how He does it! He speaks through other people, like you, and He speaks through my Bible. I guessed that He has a whole lot of other ways that He can talk to us if we just listen, just like you said." "I heard Him again and I just started thanking Him that He had answered me and I thanked Him for my life, and for His son Christ, and for you, Miss Victoria and for everything I could think of. My prayer just kept getting longer. I was so excited that every time I tried to get up off of my knees, I would think of something or someone else who I was thankful for. I felt happy again for the first time in so very long." "Thank you so much ma'am for helping me," he said.

"To God be all the glory for He has revealed this to you, Aidan, I was just the vessel that He allowed to help open your Spirit eyes," Victoria told him. Then Aidan told Victoria that he never wanted God's voice to go away again.

Victoria sat back and looked at Aidan for a moment and then she couldn't stop the tears from sliding down her face. "Aidan," She said, "I just want to thank you so much for sharing this with me; you have made my day, young man. I will admit that my weekend was a bit trying, but Abba Father knew I needed to hear this and so He led you to tell me your experience so that through you, Aidan, my day would be brighter.

So now you can see more of how God works. He used you to bring me good news, just like He used me to give you The Good News." "He is so good," Victoria shouted. "He sure is" Aidan chimed in. Then they both were laughing. "Listen Aidan, I want you to read the 14th chapter of John in your New

Testament, and memorize verses 15 thru 18." She told him that God would never leave him and as long as He is invited to stay. He will stay close; so close that we are able to be aware of His constant presence.

When Aidan left Victoria's office, they were both joyful. Victoria lifted her hands and said out loud. **The JOY of the Lord is my strength!** Victoria felt as if a heavy weight had been lifted from her shoulder and so she sang. "Joyful, joyful, Lord I adore You"...."You are Great, You do miracles so great!"

John 14
The Way, the Truth, and the Life

"Let not your heart be troubled; you believe in God, believe also in Me. 2 In My Father's house are many mansions; if it were not so, I would have told you. I go to prepare a place for you. 3 And if I go and prepare a place for you, I will come again and receive you to Myself; that where I am, there you may be also. 4 And where I go you know, and the way you know."5 Thomas said to Him, "Master, we do not know where You are going, and how can we know the way?"6 Jesus said to him, "I am the way, the truth, and the life. No one comes to the Father except through Me. 7 "If you had known Me, you would have known My Father also; and from now on you know Him and have seen Him." 8 Philip said to Him, "Master, show us the Father, and it is sufficient for us." 9 Jesus said to him, "Have I been with you so long, and yet you have not known Me, Philip? He who has seen Me has seen the Father; so how can you say, 'Show us the Father'? 10 Do you not believe that I am in the Father, and the Father in Me? The words that I speak to you I do not speak on My own authority; but the Father who dwells in Me does the works. 11 Believe Me that I am in the

Father and the Father in Me, or else believe Me for the sake of the works themselves.

The Answered Prayer

12 "Most assuredly, I say to you, he who believes in Me, the works that I do he will do also; and greater works than these he will do, because I go to My Father. 13 And whatever you ask in My name, that I will do, that the Father may be glorified in the Son. 14 If you ask] anything in My name, I will do it.

Christ Promises Another Helper

15 "If you love Me, keep My commandments. 16 And I will pray the Father, and He will give you another Helper, that He may abide with you forever— 17 the Spirit of truth, whom the world cannot receive, because it neither sees Him nor knows Him; but you know Him, for He dwells with you and will be in you. 18 I will not leave you orphans; I will come to you.

Indwelling of the Father and the Son

19 "A little while longer and the world will see Me no more, but you will see Me. Because I live, you will live also. 20 At that day you will know that I am in My Father, and you in Me, and I in you. 21 He who has My commandments and keeps them, it is he who loves Me. And he who loves Me will be loved by My Father, and I will love him and manifest Myself to him." 22 Judas (not Iscariot) said to Him, "Lord, how is it that You will manifest Yourself to us, and not to the world?" 23 Jesus answered and said to him, "If anyone loves Me, he will keep My word; and My Father will love him, and We will come to him and make Our home with him. 24 He who does not love Me does not keep My words; and the word which you hear is not Mine but the Father's who sent Me. The Gift of His Peace 25 "These things I

have spoken to you while being present with you. 26 But the Helper, the Holy Spirit, whom the Father will send in My name, He will teach you all things, and bring to your remembrance all things that I said to you. 27 Peace I leave with you, My peace I give to you; not as the world gives do I give to you. Let not your heart be troubled, neither let it be afraid. 28 You have heard Me say to you, 'I am going away and coming back to you.' If you loved Me, you would rejoice because I said, 'I am going to the Father,' for My Father is greater than I. 29 "And now I have told you before it comes, that when it does come to pass, you may believe. 30 I will no longer talk much with you, for the ruler of this world is coming, and he has nothing in Me. 31 But that the world may know that I love the Father, and as the Father gave Me commandment, so I do. Arise, let us go from here.

Caleb
Monday at 4:00pm

Now Victoria felt as if she had gotten a burst of new life. Abba, You are so merciful and kind," she thought aloud. Just then Caleb came strolling through the door, hands in his pockets as usual, but this time Victoria noticed the pensive look on his face and thought, "Uh oh, I hope he is not being transferred again to another foster home. He has been happy there and he is just too old to be shifted again." She remembered how good she thought the farm would be and how nice the Taylors had sounded when Reverend Trolli had told her about them. "YAHU'ah, please help Caleb to know for himself, that he isn't sorry and that he will make a difference, help him to know You more please." Victoria always prayed this prayer for him. "Good evening, Caleb," Victoria spoke softly because she wasn't sure what the look was about. She did know that after her session with Aidan, she could handle whatever Caleb was going through.

Caleb headed for the chair, head down, as was the norm for him, as he looked up and said hi, she thought she saw a hint of a smile. And had she detected just a little more pep in his step as opposed to the usual dragging of his feet?

"So, how was your weekend, young man?" Victoria asked with a light smile. "It was pretty good ma'am," Caleb returned her smile, however, it was more of a toothy grin, as if he had a big secret he couldn't wait to tell. "I see," she said, "Ok so do you care to elaborate, or will you continue to grin and keep me in suspense?" She smiled again, this time she was amused because she just knew something good must have happened to him. She saw no trace of Caleb's usual frown with brows creased together. He had a look with some type of evident gratification in that wide smile he was now wearing. "Ok now Caleb, she said, you look like the cat who swallowed the canary. What's going on?"

Caleb sat straight and tall, "Miss Victoria, Sunday after church, I went to the youth center to see Rev. Tee, only because I know he goes there after church." "You see, I had some questions to ask that just couldn't wait until I saw you today," Caleb, said, now looking quite thoughtful again. He began telling her all of what Reverend Tee and he had talked about, his relationship with The Most High and how they had prayed.

"Miss Victoria, you ain't never gonna believe what happened to me when I went back to that farm. It was like a miracle, and I'm still trying to comprehend that it happened to me."

He began to re-live his rooftop experience and all the events that had taken place after that, with Mr. Mike and the barn and ambulance. He even told her how he had to put the other boys to bed and then got them up and packed their lunches and fixed their breakfast before school this morning. Miss Rose was still at the hospital but she had called late last night to give him instructions. She had told him how proud of him she was and that she knew he could handle this morning's chores. He had to feed chickens, and give the cow and horse some grain and fresh straw. Then he had to put stamps on the right bills put them in the mailbox and lift up the flag on his way to the bus stop. By the end of his story Caleb's grin had grown into the biggest smile that Victoria had seen in any of the young people so far. He was showing just about every tooth he had.

Victoria sat back reflecting on Caleb's words and began to thank God but not only for Caleb's victory but for allowing all this good news from Aidan and Caleb after the past weekend's events. Tears of joy ran down her face and as they did, Caleb began his own praises and tears. He knew something new had happened in his heart. He hadn't felt anything when he first said the Sinner's Prayer with Reverend Tee or the rededication prayer with Victoria. Now he was beginning to understand this new thing in his life. Victoria thought back on the times when Caleb had tried to deceive her and how he had carried around that prideful spirit that she knew so well. My, how this young man had changed and turned his life around. In five short weeks, he was now studying for his GED and had started taking several of the online Bible school correspondence classes. He had advanced further than all of the other nineteen clients. Victoria's only concern was that he was doing this for himself and not to show Aunt Kathy or anyone else. She studied him for a moment before she spoke, "Caleb, listen. The only other person, besides yourself, you need to be concerned with pleasing is Christ our Savior." She had expressed this to him many times when he would say, "I have to show them all that I'm not so "sorry" after all."

"Caleb, she said in a low voice as she handed him tissue, I just need to know if you are doing this for yourself now." He looked up and said, "Truthfully Miss Victoria, I was trying to prove to everyone else that I ain't "sorry" that I wasn't "a no good boy"; but at some point, I started to just want it for me, I don't even know when it happened." Caleb opened up to Victoria all the things that he had experienced in the last few weeks. He told her how he had read **Psalm 139** and when he saw **verses 23 and 24**, he felt as if this might help him. "**Search me, O God, and know my heart; Try me, and know my anxieties; And see if there is any wicked way in me, and lead me in the way everlasting.**" "Once I read that, ma'am, I couldn't get it out of my mind, so I would say it and pray it as often as it came to me." Then he told her how that night on the roof top, "Just before I had heard Him call me, those verses came to me and I saw all of my life before, I knew that, Christ had changed me somewhere in these last five weeks." "I had been trying so hard pretending to be Mr. Tough guy before, when God showed me just how much better I was when I was just being Caleb, with His help." "I'm His, Miss Victoria, just like you always said, I had to let go of pride and anger and let The Father take care of it." "Thank you so much, ma'am. You and Reverend Tee saved my life." He told her that he knew that God had taken care of the bad stuff, but he also knew that he had to make the effort to keep checking his heart, so the Holy Spirit would continue to lead him in the way that is everlasting. Caleb smiled, and

Victoria said, "I am so proud of you for getting that revelation with the guidance of our Helper and because you were seeking God, He revealed it to you." "That came through your own personal relationship with Him, Caleb. I never gave you those verses in Psalms. The Spirit led you there so that He could show you who "Caleb" is and who you belong to, and then fix the stony places in your heart, to replace them with a heart of flesh." A heart pliable for God to use. Victoria gave Caleb this scripture in **Ezekiel 36:26 "I will give you a new heart and put a new spirit within you; I will take the heart of stone out of your flesh and give you a heart of flesh"** and she told him to study it. She promised that she would explain that more and that their next sessions would be more on the Holy Spirit and the role He plays in our lives. They prayed and Caleb left.

Chapter 14 – Discoveries

Victoria
That evening

Glad to be home at last, Victoria had kicked off her shoes and slid into her work out clothes. As she walked on the treadmill, thinking about today's events, she felt as if God had really blessed her with a wonderful gift. She knew that she was getting through to these kids. She began, thinking on her dream of how they had dried up like the passages in **Ezekiel 37 verses 9 and 10** and how the Spirit had encouraged her to speak openly to these young people. **"Also He said to me, 'Prophesy to the breath, prophesy son of man, and say to the breath, thus says the Most High: Come from the four winds, O breath and breathe on these slain that they may live.' So I prophesied as He commanded me, and breath came into them, and they lived, and stood upon their feet as an exceeding great army."** The dry bones were beginning to live again! She would continue to prophecy to them and they would become a great army for the Lord.

Stepping off the treadmill and heading to the shower, Victoria then began thinking on what she would have for her dinner, when the phone rang. She thought to herself, "Now who would be calling the house phone, and not my cell?" "Hello, she spoke cheerfully into the speaker." "Mrs. Victoria Hutchinson?" came the voice on the other end. "Yes, this is Victoria Hutchinson," she said, heart thumping faster than usual. The young lady on the other end instructed her to hold the line for Dr. Massey. Victoria held the line until she heard the voice of Dr. Massey, which to her resembled the voice of the actress

Gabriella London, with a type of raspy but feminine appeal to it. "Victoria, we need to talk about the results of your mammogram," She said, in a "matter of fact" tone. Now Victoria's heart was really pounding; Was the lump she had found last week, still there, and was it that of great concern? She thought to herself. When Dr. Massey spoke, she said, "The lump is there Victoria, soothing her voice, but we really need to address your options, can you come in to my office tomorrow?" Victoria told the doctor that she had appointments up till 2:00 tomorrow. They made the appointment for 3:15, she hung up the phone and sunk into the recliner.

Her appetite was gone now, replaced with a bitter taste that she couldn't describe. Victoria now visualized old man **Fear** hovering in the recesses of her thoughts. "Wait just a minute," she spoke out loud as the angel of the Lord rose up in her spirit and mind. "The devil is a LIAR, "**God has not given me a spirit of fear but of power, love, and of sound mind.**" She quoted **2 Timothy 1:7, 1 Peter 2:24 "by His stripes I'm healed"** and every other scripture she could remember she was now praying, in English, but mostly in her heavenly language through the Holy Spirit. **Romans 8:11** now came into her mind, "**But if the Spirit of Him who raised Christ from the dead dwells in you, He who raised the Anointed One from the dead will also give life to your mortal bodies through His Spirit who dwells in you.**" She then ended her prayer with **2 Peter 1:3**... "**as His divine power has given to us all things that pertain to life and godliness, through the knowledge of Him who called us by glory and virtue.**" She was at peace and smiling about the excellent testimonies from the two young men earlier today.

Victoria knew that this new attack on her body was because she was making progress with the youth through the Holy Spirit. As she stepped into the shower, she spoke aloud again, "Well now devil, I am not about to let you steal them back." After finishing her shower, and getting into her pajamas, she marched straight back into her bedroom to pull out her home files. She began fervent effectual prayers for all twenty young people and a special healing prayer for Stephanie. After praying for the youth, she prayed for herself "Father, I submit myself to you in prayer. You, are called Jahovah Rapha and You are the healer. Because I know You to be merciful and just, and because I know that my body is healed and whole now, by 1 Peter 2:24, it is in Christ's name that I send these prayers and "YOUR WORD out into the atmosphere." "For according to **Psalm 107:20, "You sent your word to heal me, and these words will not return void**." "With one last quote on it Father, I speak this word, and I believe I receive it as fact according to my faith in your promises," **"So shall My word be that goes forth from My mouth; It shall not return to Me void, But it shall accomplish what I please, And it shall prosper in the thing for which I sent it" Isaiah 55:11.** By this word and my prayer I call it done, no lumps, no tumors, no cancer. Be gone now! I pray Your Word back to You Father in the name of Jesus of Nazareth the Anointed One, Amen and Amen." With that, Victoria decided she needed to eat something before 7:30. She walked purposefully into the kitchen, with her head held as high as she could hold it. "So NOW **Mister Fear** you can go right ahead and take your flight." **"Therefore submit unto GOD. Resist the devil and he will flee from you" James 4:7.**

Tuesday

Victoria had finished her appointments and it was now 2:15 as she walked across the church parking lot to her car. She was thinking of how her own mother who had fought breast cancer, had a double mastectomy, was in remission for five years and when the cancer came back it was in the pancreas. The chemo was too much for her, she died of heart complications after a bout with pneumonia.

After Victoria and her dad, Victor, had found her again, they both had been strong for Momma up till the very end. They had fought for her in prayer and in the physical, when one day she finally told them that she was tired and didn't want to fight anymore. She had said she was ready to go home. Victoria resisted for several days but the last heart attack and pneumonia had taken its toll on Lillian Graham and she was suffering. Victoria knew she had to let go. As much as she struggled with the thought of not having her mom around for the second time in her life, she hated seeing her this way. Victoria finally told Lillian that she would be ok, and the very same night she passed on. Oh, how Victoria longed to talk to her Momma right now, if only it were possible. However, she couldn't allow the enemy to think he had a foothold, so she continued on confessing the Word of God's promises. She reached the car, got in, and started it up then headed south to Dr. Massey's office.

As the doctor walked into the exam room, Victoria felt a bit of anxiety, she immediately said, "The blood of Jesus is against you, you **fear** demon, I resist you by the strength of Christ, The Anointed One!" "I beg your pardon," Dr. Massey said. Victoria told her that she was praying out loud. "Well, Victoria, there's no need to be afraid or think the worst yet," Dr. Massey reassured. Victoria said, "I'm not afraid, I was just praying and confessing wholeness." Doctor Massey briefly stared a faraway look, it was as if she looked right through her to a different place. She seemed all of a sudden to shake a thought away and began explaining the process of biopsy and what might or might not happen following the procedure. She also explained that the biopsy could be performed on a Saturday for her convenience. Victoria said she would like it done as soon as possible, and since Dr. Massey had slots available this Saturday, Victoria decided she would take the 8:00 am slot.

On the way home, Victoria continued to thank Abba Father in advance for total healing and complete wholeness standing on the word. "And as the scripture tells me in **1 Peter 2:24** of the Amplified Bible" **"He personally carried our sins in His body on the cross [willingly offering Himself on it, as on an altar of sacrifice], so that we might die to sin [becoming immune from the penalty and power of sin] and live for righteousness; for by His wounds you [who believe] have been healed."**

At home that evening, Victoria read excerpts Dr. Massey had given her for the procedure: For many biopsies, you'll get an injection to numb the area of the breast to be biopsied.

Fine-needle aspiration biopsy
This is the simplest type of breast biopsy and will be used to evaluate the lump that was felt during a clinical breast exam. For the procedure, you will lie on a table. While steadying the lump with one hand, your doctor uses the other hand to direct a very thin needle into the lump. The needle is attached to a

syringe that can collect a sample of cells or fluid from the lump. Fine-needle aspiration is a quick way to distinguish between a fluid-filled cyst and a solid mass and, possibly, to avoid a more invasive biopsy procedure. If, however, the mass is solid, a tissue sample will be obtained.

Core needle biopsy

This type of breast biopsy may be used to assess a breast lump that's visible on a mammogram or ultrasound or that your doctor feels (palpates) during a clinical breast exam. A radiologist or surgeon uses a thin, hollow needle to remove tissue samples from the breast mass, most often using ultrasound guidance. Several samples, each about the size of a grain of rice, are collected and analyzed to identify features indicating the presence of disease. Depending on the location of the mass, other imaging techniques, such as a mammogram or MRI, may be used to guide the positioning of the needle to obtain the tissue sample.

After a breast biopsy

With all types of breast biopsy except a surgical biopsy, you'll go home with only bandages and an ice pack over the biopsy site. Although you should take it easy for the rest of the day, you'll be able to resume your normal activities within a day. Bruising is common after core needle biopsy procedures. To ease pain and discomfort after a breast biopsy, you may take a non-aspirin pain reliever containing acetaminophen (Tylenol, others) and apply a cold pack as needed to reduce swelling. If you have a surgical biopsy, you'll likely have stitches (sutures) to care for. You will go home the same day of your procedure and you can resume usual activities the next day. Your health care team will tell you how to protect your stitches. (Excerpt paraphrase from the Mayo Clinic procedure details).

Father, I thank You in advance that there is NO fluid-filled cyst, no solid mass is in my body in Christ's name, that all that was there is dissolved, that I am healed and whole according to 1 Peter 2:24 Amen. Victoria then laid her hand where she had felt the lump and quoted scripture after scripture for healing and wholeness. After that she stood and walked to her desk and wrote as she spoke these words: **I decree and declare this day that there are no lumps or masses in my body in Christ's name.** *She then took a piece of tape, walked into the bathroom and taped the paper to her mirror. Now she knew the first thing in the morning she would see this and declare it; She would also place the decree on her desk at work so it was visible to her during the day and each day she would declare it many times.*

Victoria read her Bible carefully picking out faith-filled words to type up and place in areas that she saw throughout the day. She would repeat faith-filled words and healing verses over her body daily as she continued to pray for Stephanie. She had also kept contact with Mable and Charity concerning Stephanie's progress, only speaking to Stephanie once to remind her of their session on Wednesday at 4:00.

Stephanie had regained feeling in her legs and had just a few headaches throughout the day. Charity had told Victoria that Stephanie would be moving to the rehabilitation center next to the hospital and would start her first day of aggressive physical therapy tomorrow morning, 9:00, after breakfast and again in the afternoon, 1:30, after lunch and evening at 6:30 after dinner. It was estimated that Stephanie would be there at the rehab center for at least four weeks to start, and then come in as an outpatient later, depending upon her progress.

Chapter 15 – Shepherding

Stephanie
Wednesday

Stephanie was sore and irritated by the time Victoria arrived at the rehab center. She had spoken with a friend earlier, who had said that Rick was either out or getting out on bond. She was nervous and fidgety every time she heard someone walk down the hallway toward her room. Mable had assured her daughter that she had a restricted visitor list which meant anyone who came asking to see her had to be on the list and show ID to get in. Besides there were guards on duty at the front desk around the clock. Once past the metal detectors, visitors had to go to the guard desk to get in. Aside from the issue with Rick last week, there had apparently been issues in the past causing the rehab center to take extra security precautions and since last week's incident with Rick the hospital had also put extra security precautions in place.

Victoria was feeling a bit troubled because she had been just a little distracted that morning with her other clients but she had decided she would be attentive with Stephanie, after all she was her last appointment for the day. She had walked into the rehab center and had been bombarded by security at the door asking the purpose of her visit; they then directed her to a kiosk where a security officer and a county sheriff were seated. They wanted to see her picture I.D. as they asked who she had come to visit. She felt a bit irritated but she then recalled that Mable had called to tell her the rehab was on high security alert after learning of Rick's release. She also told Victoria that whenever Stephanie was released they would have to get a restraining order against "that monster," as Mable had labeled Rick.

Now Victoria and Stephanie sat face to face in Stephanie's room for the first time in days at this rehabilitation center. The child still looked pretty battered and is more fidgety than ever, poor thing, Victoria thought to herself. "Well now, Stephanie, how are you feeling today?" Stephanie just looked at Victoria for a moment then she said, "I don't know" as tears began streaming down her face. She started sobbing, long and deep until she was out of breath. Victoria tried to console her, when at last she just began to pray, "Father God, You are also called El Roi because you are Omniscient and You see and know all things. You and only You can know the very depths of our despair. I ask You now, dear Father to touch Stephanie, soothe her, comfort her, and give her the peace that Christ has promised to us. Father, we need Your strength for we know that Your strength is perfect in our weakness. Please, help us to know also that You have promised to never leave us or forsake us, so we thank You now for Your presence in our lives and we ask now for Your guardian angels to be dispatched to bear us up, so that we stay forever inside Your hedge of protection. In the name of The Anointed One, the Christ, Amen."

When she opened her eyes, Stephanie had stopped crying and was looking at her very intently. "What's wrong?" Victoria asked. "Nothing is wrong ma'am, everything is right when you pray like that, she replied. "I tried to pray and all I could think of was the prayer I learned as a little girl at Vacation Bible School." Stephanie said it as if she didn't understand. Victoria then asked her if she could hear the prayer, so Stephanie shyly spoke.

> *"The Lord is my Shepherd; I shall not want.*
> *He makes me to lie down in green pastures;*
> *He leads me beside the still waters. He restores my soul;*
> *He leads me in the paths of righteousness for His name's sake.*
> *Even, though I walk through the valley in the shadow of death, I will fear no evil; For You are with me; Your rod and Your staff, they comfort me.*
> *You prepare a table before me in the presence of my enemies; You anoint my head with oil; My cup runs over. Surely goodness and mercy shall follow me, all the days of my life; And I will dwell in the house of the Most High… Forever."*

Stephanie had her head down as if she was embarrassed. "That was beautiful, the **23rd Psalm**," Victoria said. Stephanie looked up. She told Victoria that she really hadn't said it much since she was little because her step brothers had always laughed at her when she tried to say it when they came to hurt her. She said she thought it didn't work and that God didn't really hear her. "So that's why I stopped saying it, but since that night with Rick, I can't get it out of my mind, so I keep saying it." 'I figured if I said it enough, that He might hear me now."

Victoria began to minister to Stephanie instead of counseling her. She told her how God had heard her but how the devil had tricked her into thinking that He wasn't listening. She began to tell her that He talks back to us and tells us through our Spirit man, things we should and should not do. She told her that many times we don't listen because our flesh doesn't want to listen to the right things, and even though we know things are not good for us we continue to self-destruct.

Victoria then explained free will and why the Father is a loving God, He would never force us to do what's right. "You see Stephanie, we have to choose the right path when He speaks to us. The right path is narrow and straight but there is always room on it for all who will follow it." "Does that make sense to you?" "Yes ma'am," Stephanie said, now that you explained it, it makes perfect sense, I can remember some of those times I heard warnings and didn't listen; there was always trouble at the end of that."

Victoria talked a little more, then she told Stephanie that if she wanted to learn more she would help her. "Oh yes ma'am, I want to hear everything now, I know I need God, and I really need His help." The scripture passages that Victoria gave Stephanie to study were: **John 14:1-4** the words of the Savior Himself **"Let not your heart be troubled; you believe in God, believe also in Me. In My Father's house are many mansions, if it were not so, I would have told you. I go to prepare a place for you. And if I go and prepare a place for you, I will come again and receive you to Myself; that where I am, there you may be also. And where I go you know, and the way you know."** Then verses **25-27 "These things I have spoken to you while being present with you. But the Helper, the Holy Spirit, whom the Father will send in My name, He will teach you all things, and bring to your remembrance all things that I said to you. Peace, I leave with you, My peace I give to you; not as the world gives do I give to you. Let not your heart be troubled, neither let it be afraid."**

"When I come back next week, we'll talk all about those passages and the role the Holy Spirit plays in our lives. Okay." Victoria said. Stephanie said, "Okay, and guess what?" "That headache I had for the last few days is gone," she said smiling. Victoria smiled too. She said another short prayer before she left. She then found Mable to let her know she was leaving.

As she walked to her car to go home, she had a strange feeling, as if an evil force was watching her. While she was driving, the feeling wouldn't go away and she kept praying as she continued seeing the same car headlights in her rearview mirror, how she longed for the time change to go forward, so it wasn't dark so early. Victoria began to pray harder, asking Holy Spirit for guidance. She turned the corner three blocks before her home and the car behind also turned. That's when she saw that unmistakable "Playa 1" on the license plate as another car's lights shined on it. Victoria then followed the road which she knew lead to the police precinct about a mile or so down. She was wearing her Bluetooth so as she drove she dialed 911. She briefly explained the situation and told where she was, she gave the operator her car make, model, color and plate number and the plate number of the Toyota that was following her. After two blocks she saw a squad car parked at the intersection, she stopped at the STOP sign then proceeded. The car that was still behind her at the sign continued through also. As soon as the car followed, she saw the police car in her mirror as they turned on the blue lights and turned the corner behind the car. Another officer was at the next corner and he followed her to the precinct. She sighed a breath she had been involuntarily holding. She went inside and was told to take a seat in a room, shortly after that she saw two officers come into the lobby with Rick in tow, they had him handcuffed. She knew that she had been right when she told the operator who the person following her might be. She could envision all those hateful spirits that used Rick: fear, anger, jealousy, hate and a host of various imps followed this young man. His facial expression was so contorted that Victoria could just imagine his stony heart.

Her stomach turned and she almost lurched at the sight of him. "Abba Father! My Savior, I thank You for discernment and for Your divine protection, and for the angels that bear me up, in Christ's name." Victoria closed her eyes and exhaled the breath she had been holding again.

The two officers entered the room where Victoria was sitting. The one calmly asked her if she had seen the young man they had brought in. When she answered yes, they asked if she knew him and she said, "Yes but not personally." They told her they would need to take a statement; after they took her statement they asked if she wanted to file a restraining order and press charges. "Yes, I think that would be best," She replied. She thought to herself, "I filed a restraining order once before and was still continually harassed, but I didn't know about dispatching my angels back then or how to pray effective prayers. God had still been there, because it would have been a lot worse had He not been."

Victoria smiled as she finished the paperwork, "God has me and He has Stephanie." She began quoting scripture as she left the station and headed home. No weapons formed against me shall prosper. For God has given His angels charge over me. He has not given me a Spirit of fear but of power, love and of sound mind ….and she went on and on like this all the way home knowing that her protectors surrounded her. The officers had explained that they would be holding Rick on harassment charges and the judge would set his bail tomorrow morning. She could also submit her application for a restraining order at the courthouse. These police officers were familiar with Rick and told her they knew he had many friends and ill-gotten resources. Yes, his bail would most likely be posted as soon as it was set, but that Rick was already being watched for his illegal activities. She had told them thank you and that she would be fine now.

Victoria knew that Rick wouldn't come up against her again because she didn't fear him or the demons that drove him. Tonight, she would pray for him that The Most High would grant grace for him to accept salvation-before he destroyed himself through his unsavory deeds and those hateful spirits that led him.

Chapter 16 – Prophesying

Gloria
Thursday at 3:00pm

Today had been a struggle for Victoria, after her encounter with Rick last night, but she had asked the Father for strength and she was feeling better now. Victoria had purposely set a second appointment this week for Gloria. She seemed to have made less progress than any of the others as far as trying or wanting to develop a personal relationship with God. Only two of the original 20 had stopped coming to their sessions, altogether. This saddened Victoria, but she continued to pray for them; it reminded her of her dream in the valley where some of the individuals didn't stand or drink from their cups. However, Victoria remained optimistic continuing in prayer for those two.

"Hi there, Miss Victoria," Gloria said beaming. Victoria jumped from her reverie when Gloria's voice sounded in her ears. Victoria looked at her watch, 3:56. "Well will wonders never cease, not only are you on time but you are early. "I'm so proud of you Gloria! 'Y te ves hermosa hoy!" **(And don't you look beautiful today)** "Gracias a ti también" **(Thank you and you too.)** Gloria had on business casual clothes and wore light make-up, which was out of the ordinary for her. She looked like someone who worked in an office, instead of the usual greasy spoon restaurant clothes and heavy makeup she'd always worn.

Gloria literally pranced over to the chair and as she sat she immediately began explaining. OMG Miss Victoria you will never began to guess what has happened to me in the last few days. "Do tell," Victoria said as she sat back smiling. "First off, Gloria started, 'my cousin Millie, I mean Milagras, she don't like me callin' her Millie you know, like you don't like me callin' you Vicky.' "Anyhow, she gave me these clothes and she put on my makeup, because she said I wear too much." I had a job interview today at the electric company, for the receptionist position, I had applied online two months ago and I kept calling to check because it kept showing up in the job sites." Gloria went on for about five or six minutes, talking about how she gotten a second interview for tomorrow.

She talked until she finally looked at Victoria with tears in her eyes. "Oh Miss Victoria" she said blowing her nose. "I know this was God answering me." She told Victoria that she had read that whole book and she had cried because the girl "Lydia" kept talking about how she had talked to God and how He kept answering her prayers. Gloria went on about how she wanted that in her life, and about all the scripture verses in that book were for her. She told Victoria how she had looked in her Bible and read them over and over these last two days.

She had stopped crying now and was telling her story with excitement as if she had come out of a valley and was now climbing to get to the mountaintop. Gloria continued, "Miss Victoria when I prayed that first night, I put on soft music like Lydia. I prayed like that girl Lydia in the book you gave me." As Gloria took a little piece of paper out of her purse, she read this prayer "O Most High God, I thank You for who You are and for all You are doing in my life. I pray now, Father, that you forgive me for all my sins and cleanse me according to 1 John 1:9. You say there that You will forgive me and cleanse me from all the bad stuff. Father, I want You in my life and I expect You to do a good work in me. God, I want to hear Your voice and I need You to guide me to where I need to go and what I need to do. Speak to me now Most High God and help me to understand who I am and what my purpose is. In Christ's name, Amen.

Gloria looked up and said 'I added this part myself.' "Oh and God, I really would love to have that job, so what should I do my Father?" "Miss Victoria always says that You have all the answers, so please share with me O Most High. I know it is Your will for me and your plan is for me to live Victorious and have hope and a future like in Jeremiah 29:11. I do love You Father and even if I haven't been the best before, I'm ready to do my best now. Amen"

'That's what I said Miss Victoria and when I got off my knees I sat in the chair and waited just like Lydia did in the book. After a while, I thought I was asleep but I was just in and out like some kind of transformer was happening, it looked like a fog in my house you know." Victoria smiled and told her, "That word is transformation." "Ok, transformation. Anyways, I heard a voice in my ear telling me to call the electric place, so I said, God is that You?" No kidding either, Miss Victoria, "I heard the voice say, "I am the Holy Spirit, of Christ, who died for You… call them now." "So I walked to the phone, it felt like I was walking on feather pillows, I called the number and pushed the numbers to get to H.R. A lady answered and when I told her my name she said, 'oh my, I have your application up on my screen now, I was just about to call you.'

"Are you available to come in for an interview tomorrow morning at 10:30 and bring your resume, the one online is not real clear, and two forms of I.D.?" "I said yes ma'am I'll be there with all of that, 10:25 on the dot." The lady laughed and I laughed but I meant it." She told Victoria that she had cried when she hung up. She said she had asked the Spirit if He was still there, because I could still see the cloudiness in the room. She told Victoria that she had heard Him in her inside and He said, 'Always.' "I don't even feel angry anymore, she added. What was that cloudiness?"

After Gloria finished, Victoria sat back with tears streaming down as the electricity of Gloria's anointed testimony went from her head to her toes. She finally spoke, "Gloria, she said, out of all the people that I know, you are the only one, that I know personally, who has had this type of amazing visitation from the Spirit of the Living God. The Shekinah glory, the divine presence of Christ came and settled in your house!" "I have read it, seen it on TV. What an amazing gift to you from the Anointed One." "Now please excuse me while I praise Him. She stood, lifted her hands and sang out, "HalleluYAH, You are faithful to perform Your word, Glory to Your name!" She began to praise and Gloria was now standing with her hands raised and crying. They praised for several more minutes and Victoria came around the desk and hugged Gloria, something she hadn't done with any of the others, not even Stephanie. Then Gloria said something so amazing, "That job is mine... right Miss Victoria?"

"Maybe now the courts will let me have my little brother and baby sister," Gloria added. Victoria hugged her again, "Yes I agree, the job is yours in Christ's name. I will continue to pray about you getting your siblings." Gloria said ok to this but she was tearing up again and Victoria held her. She knew how badly Gloria wanted her siblings with her. All the girl talked about in those first sessions was getting them and bringing them to church.

Victoria gave Gloria a scripture to meditate on: **Philippians 4:13,** the first scripture she had ever given her. **"I can do all things through Christ, who strengthens me."** She told her to call after the second interview and let her know when she starts, "So I can fit your last two sessions into your new schedule. As Gloria was leaving, she turned to Victoria and said, "I guess I was a special case for God's divine presence to come to my dusty ole shack. I sure hope He scared off some of the vermin in there." They both laughed and Victoria got serious and said, "With this new job you can move and I will be there to help you.

When Gloria left, Victoria sat alone in her office meditating on Gloria's testimony. She prayed aloud, "Father God, I thank You for sending the comforter to Gloria. "I thank You Holy Spirit, for being a guide and a comforter. I thank You for Gloria's new job and for her success on the job. She's a smart girl and she will do well and excel by Your guidance." "Father, I had no idea how to get through to this complex young lady who had been abused by the very person who should've protected her. You used me to plant the seeds she needed in her heart that was all you needed from me, but you used a book of the testimony of another young person to water that seed and You sent the very Ruah Holy Spirit with the increase so that now she knows who You are. I bless Your Holy name and I will bless Your name at all times. Thank You in Christ's name, Amen. Victoria would meditate on these scripture verses. "**I planted, Apollo's watered, but God [all the while] was causing the growth. So neither is the one who plants nor the one who waters anything, but [only] God who causes the growth. He who plants and he who waters are one [in importance and esteem, working toward the same purpose]; but each will receive his own reward according to his own labor**" **1 Corinthians 3:6-8 Amplified Bible**.

Chapter 17 – Miracles

Victoria's Miracle
Saturday

Victoria arrived at the hospital at 7:45 as instructed for her biopsy. She had been laying her hands on her breast and speaking healing scripture over herself since her last visit with Dr. Massey. Victoria had not been able to find the lump for the last few days. She had also visited the intercessory prayer room several times during that week. Charity had purposefully laid hands on the area where the lump was located. She had prayed a prayer of agreement with Victoria and confessed healing over her. The women had bound the lump and loosed health and wellness over her body. Victoria had felt and confessed within herself, that she was completely healed and the lump was dissolved. Then she would be sure to decree it in writing and declare it out loud. She was confident now, she had no worries all.

When the surgeon walked in with Dr. Massey, she told Victoria that they had decided to do the **Core needle biopsy.** Dr. Massey explained again that this type of breast biopsy can be used to assess a breast lump that's visible on a mammogram or ultrasound or that your doctor feels (palpates) during a clinical breast exam. The surgeon uses a thin, hollow needle to remove tissue samples from the breast mass, most often using ultrasound guidance. Several samples, each about the size of a grain of rice, are collected and analyzed to identify features indicating the presence of disease. Depending on the location of the mass, other imaging techniques, such as a mammogram or MRI, may be used to guide the positioning of the needle to obtain the tissue sample.

While Victoria was being prepped, she informed Dr. Massey that she had not been able to feel the lump in the last three days and asked her if she could examine her again. The doctor was unimpressed; however, she did as Victoria asked. She was so astonished that she was not able to feel the mass that she had so distinctly felt before and that had appeared on the mammogram. Dr. Massey checked again and several more times before she and the surgeon discussed the findings. They were stumped so they decided on doing another ultrasound. After the ultrasound, they found no visible signs of the mass. They then told Victoria that they were sending her down for an MRI. Victoria just smiled and said ok. As she headed down for the MRI she kept smiling and thanking God for answered prayer. She had felt confident that she was going to have a good report today but she now knew that the mass had dissolved on its own by the power and promise of the Most High God. She had asked Abba Father to dissolve it, in those words, many times and after that she had begun confessing that it was dissolved with no traces of it. The whole time she laid inside that MRI tunnel she was smiling and more relaxed than she could ever remember being before.

While at home cooking later that night, Victoria thought of how Dr. Massey had said, we will call you as soon as we get the results of the MRI. Victoria smiled when she remembered the look on the doctor's face when she had told her that she already knew what the results would be. "I beg your pardon," Dr. Massey had said seeming a bit irritated that they didn't have the answers.

Victoria had been able to witness to Dr. Massey then. Although the doctor seemed skeptical, she listened then she shared that several of her colleagues had been through this type of happening and weren't able to explain it. She also shared that her younger sister, who was a lawyer, had become a believer and had been trying to convert her for over a year. Dr. Massey had looked so puzzled but Victoria just smiled and said, "You should listen to your sister, there's so much more you could be as a believing doctor.

Victoria had prayed for Dr. Massey all the way home. In between praying she kept singing the song over and over. "For You are Great… You do miracles so Great… There is no One else like You." Victoria sat down to eat. She prayed over her food and ate dinner, smiling and humming the same tune. She thought of two scripture verses, one for Dr. Massey. **1 Corinthians 3:6, "I planted, Apollo's watered, but God gave the increase,"** and one for herself, **1 John 5:14-15, "Now this is the confidence that we have in Him, that if we ask anything according to His will, He hears us. And if we know that He hears us, whatever we ask, we know that we have the petitions that we have asked of Him."**

She was now singing again, 'How Great is our God,' and then, 'How Great Thou Art,' 'Nobody Greater,' and on and on. Victoria sang in the shower, she hummed as she read and all the way until she prayed her goodnight prayer. When she laid her head on her pillow she kept smiling and singing songs of worship until she fell asleep.

Chapter 18 – No more dry bones

Gloria Maria Santiago & Victoria Hutchinson
Saturday morning at 10:00am

Victoria had been thinking and praying for Gloria Santiago a lot in the last few days. She knew in her heart that all of these young people had anger issues but, Gloria, in spite of her visit from Holy Spirit and her new relationship with Abba was having a real hard time with anger because she had not yet addressed or accepted what had happened to her sister Damaris and she hadn't forgiven her mother for her sister's death. Even though Victoria was very much involved with Stephanie and her hard issues, she still had considered Gloria her special case, because she herself had had explosive anger issues in her younger years.

Victoria began thinking back over her own life. Her father Victor had been supportive, loving, and had always taken her to church. He would teach her about the Father on High and give her life lessons. He was an intelligent and handsome man, mild mannered and soft spoken. He had a great work ethic, he knew his job well and employers loved him. Victoria's mother, however, had serious anger issues. She would slap Victoria around when her dad wasn't at home. Her mother had told her daily that she was stupid, fat and ugly, and what a big disappointment she was. She also told Victoria that she would be just like her, "A big FAT nobody!" Victoria didn't tell Victor because he worked so hard trying to support them and to please her mother, she just didn't want to cause anymore to be on his shoulders. He would say to her mother, "Lillian, just calm down honey, everything will work out." He would hold her until she calmed down. One day, soon after Victoria's 12th birthday, her mother just left them, she wrote a note that said, "I just can't do this anymore."

Victoria always blamed herself because she thought her mother hated her. She began having eruptions of anger. Victor had put her in anger management, but Victoria just refused to open up to the counselors. When Victoria was fifteen years old, one day after church, a pretty young woman approached her; her name was Hallie Houseman. Hallie was a little on the heavy side but she was beautiful. Victoria began spending a lot of time with Hallie; when Hallie had witnessed Victoria's explosive temper a couple of times. One day she told Victoria she wanted to have a serious talk with her. Hallie sat Victoria down and began asking her about her life; after Victoria cried and spilled all the beans. Hallie held her in her arms and told her she was willing to be her big sister. She also talked to Victoria about love and the importance of forgiveness. When they met to go shopping or just for after-school talks and walks in the park; they would sit and Hallie would teach and minister to Victoria everything she knew about love and forgiveness and how the role of Holy Spirit in our lives is to help us.

Victoria grew in all the areas and in her love of the Bible, every chance she had and every open moment she would devour every word. As a result Victoria was able to forgive her mother. By the time she was eighteen, she had learned where her mother was and had heard that she wasn't well. Victoria told Victor everything that had happened and they cried together. Victor apologized to Victoria for not being more attentive to her. He always knew there was a strain between his daughter and wife but he didn't know how to handle it. He just kept praying and hoping for God to help them to resolve their issues.

Lillian had agreed to see her daughter, so Victoria asked Hallie to fly out to Colorado Springs with her, for a visit with her mom. Victoria was taken aback as she walked in the door of her mother's assisted living apartment. She was so frail and her once long beautiful chestnut hair was replaced by a thin whisper of mixed gray patches. She asked the caregiver if she could be alone with Lillian.

When the young woman had left the room, Victoria said, "Hello mother, I won't ask how you are because I can see for myself." Lillian looked up at her now beautiful daughter who had slimmed down and had grown tall like her Father. Victoria had beautiful chestnut hair like Lillian's once was. Lillian began crying so Victoria immediately went to her and held her, wiping her tears and telling her how much she loved her.

Once Lillian was composed, she began apologizing to her daughter and began by saying, "Every negative thing I told you was a lie., I knew you weren't fat or ugly or stupid. You were never a disappointment, especially to Victor." "I'm ashamed to say it but, I was jealous of you, Victoria. I hated how much your father adored you, but I had no right to hit you and lie to you the way I did." "No mother should ever be jealous of her own daughter." Victoria then held Lillian in her arms and hugged her lightly because it seemed like she could feel every bone in her mother's body and that she might fracture something if she held her as tight as she really wanted to. "It's ok mom, I know God now and I forgive you." Daddy also told me how he had gotten you away from your own abusive mother, and he'd married you because he loved you and he hated how you were treated by her. He said your mother had said no to the marriage because Victor was too old. Even though he was only six years older than you.

Because you were eighteen, you could give your own consent and you did. Victoria and Lillian talked for several hours until Lillian's pain medication really kicked in and she could no longer stay awake. Victoria left and said she would come tomorrow before her flight. True to her word, she came to say goodbye to Lillian. Victoria cried on the plane and Hallie cried with her. Hallie held Victoria's hand and stroked it lightly with her other hand. "The pain will go away my friend, I promise. Our heavenly Father will dry these tears in time." Hallie comforted Victoria as much as she could.

 For months after that visit, Victoria would send Lillian a little money from time to time; she worked at the drug store and had started classes so she didn't have a lot to send. She called Lillian on the phone as much and as often as she could. Her father, Victor, was helping with the cost of Lillian's care aide and since they never divorced, he hadn't taken her off of his insurance at work. Although Lillian hadn't been using it, they were able to use it for her hospital stays and hospice after she had gotten worse. During one conversation between Lillian and Victoria, she had led her mother in a prayer to rededicate her life to Christ and to forgive her own mother who had died years ago.

Two weeks later, Lillian passed away. Although Victoria was sad that she didn't have more time with her mom, and she was losing her for the second time, she was still happy that her mother no longer had to suffer but mostly that she would no longer have to have any bad memories. She knew that her mother was now safe with the Most High. The phone rang and it seemed a lot louder than usual. It had pulled Victoria from her reverie.

Answering the call and just a bit overwhelmed that it was Gloria Santiago, after she was just comparing her life to Gloria's, Victoria had listened and agreed to meet with her because she sounded so desperate. "Ok Gloria can you come to my office tomorrow at 2:00? I don't normally do this on Saturday but I'll be there tying up some paperwork. Besides, my week is jam-packed so I can't schedule you in." Gloria agreed they said their goodbyes and hung up.

Victoria prayed, and wondered what the urgency was. She asked the Father to give her divine discernment and the right words to help her feisty young friend. Well now Abba, no wonder she was on my heart so heavy; You knew she was going to call and you know why too, You are so Awesome Omniscient Elohim!

The next day as Victoria went about her morning, she wondered and prayed. She left for her office at 9:00 am to get started on cleaning up her files, among other chores. She suspected that Gloria would be late which had been her typical pattern. So when the buzzer when off at 1:40, Victoria nearly jumped out of her skin.

She composed herself as she headed for the front door of the church. 'Maybe it's UPS' she thought to herself. She was so surprised to see Gloria standing there that she fumbled clumsily with the lock on the door. "Gloria" she exclaimed, you're early." They both laughed as they walked talking about all the times she had been late, Gloria's excuses, and how they had bumped heads at their first meeting. "Boy you told me off good about calling you Vicky," Gloria rambled. Once they were in Victoria's office they went into the professional role of Counselor and Client.

Victoria: Ok Gloria what's going on these days and what was so urgent? You've held me in suspense once again.

Gloria: Miss Victoria, I don't want to be angry anymore! I have asked Christ into my heart. I do all that I know to serve Him and keep His commandments; I just don't understand why I still get so ANGRY!!! I really don't want to be this way anymore.

Victoria: Hmmm, Did you bring your Bible with you?

Gloria: Yes, I have it here in my purse, but I just want an answer about this anger and these outbursts that sometimes come out of nowhere. I don't think the Bible is going to have an answer for me.

Victoria: Now that's where you're wrong. Have you been reading it?

Gloria: Well... sometimes I do but I don't understand it

Victoria: Uh huh, just as I thought. Here take this pen and paper so you can write down the verses I give you. Listen Gloria, the Bible has an answer for every question you have. You **must** not only read it, you have to study it, meditate on it and ask The Holy Spirit to help you when you study. He is our helper. Christ sent Him to us to walk beside us and to help us with everything. He is actually called the Paraclete. In Latin that means advocate or helper. Ruakh HA'Kodesh (Holy Spirit) is also known as our comforter which is what Jesus called Him in John 16:7 when He was explaining to the disciples why He had to go away and how important the Spirit is. Holy Spirit is the peace Christ promised in John 14:27. One other thing I mentioned that it is very important is to study and meditate. In 2 Timothy 2:15, Paul stressed to Timothy the importance of studying and being approved, and how to rightly divide the words in the Bible so you know it for yourself. We'll talk more on rightly dividing the word later.

Gloria: Wow, you sure know your stuff. So can you show me where the Bible tells me how to get rid of my anger?

Victoria: Indeed I can if you are willing to continue some after-hours sessions.

Gloria: I want it so badly Ms. Victoria, I hate the outbursts and I don't want to lose my job. I really like my job. My bosses have been very nice and have given me another chance. I exploded on two different co-workers, two separate times and I'm lucky to still be there. I had to agree to it so they set me up with anger management only because they feel I'm very good at my job. A hard worker and I'm a "quick study", they always say that. Yesterday my immediate supervisor called me into her office to ask me about my progress in anger management. I told her it was coming along well. What I didn't tell her is that I'm very careful at work and I pray when I feel it coming on, but outside of work it happens more often. I need more help, Ms.

Victoria, that's why I called you. I knew our regular special financed sessions were over, but I think I can pay your fee for more help if you give me a payment plan.

Victoria: Well, we can discuss my fee later. Right now I just need to show you how studying your Bible can teach you how to get that angry spirit to leave you alone. Ok.

Gloria: Ok

Victoria: Well now, let's see, we talked about needing to study the Word more but the main things are getting some past issues out into the open and then we can talk about what the Bible says about the situation.

Over the next six weeks Victoria and Gloria would discuss how her mother had blamed her for her father leaving them and told her she had to go to work selling herself. Her father had really gone back to Puerto Rico to work with his brother in construction. Her mother smoked, drank, did drugs and cussed at her from morning till night. She spent the money Poppy would send home on drugs and alcohol, she even sold her food stamps. Gloria remembered how her mother had prostituted her at age 13, plastering her face with make-up and making her take these little pills every day. After a week of pills, Gloria's mother would then call various men to come to pick
Gloria up and force her to do unspeakable acts with them. It was awful, the first few times she threw up for days afterward, she hurt all over and her legs and arms were bruised. She cried and begged her mother not to send her but it never ended. At first a couple of times a week was all; but later, every day, sometimes twice.

Gloria cried when she talked about her older sister. Poor Damaris was only twelve when she started out. Her mother had told her the same thing about it being her fault that her Poppy was gone. Damaris would tell Gloria that she hated "Mommy" and that she would run away and make a lot of money as an actress. She told Gloria she would come back for her, but she never did, she was dead. Gloria had been angry with Damaris for leaving her with "Mommy" and then leaving her forever. Gloria was angry with her father because he had left.

Gloria voiced how horrified she was when Poppy returned after he found out about Damaris' death and he had learned that Gloria was on the streets too.

There had been a big argument and her mother had stabbed her father. There was blood everywhere, he was in the hospital for weeks and almost died. The doctors said he was lucky; another half inch and his heart would have been history. Gloria told Victoria how in court several neighbors testified about how Mommy had bragged that if he came back she would stab him right in the heart. So she got an attempted murder charge. Gloria was angry with her mother for a lot of reasons; she had been just plain old angry with every one of them and everyone else, even God.

After Victoria and Gloria went over all these things, Victoria began the healing process by explaining again about the Holy Spirit and His role in our lives. That He, being the third person of the Trinity, spoke only to God on our behalf and He was to help us to pray and to comfort us along the way; to walk beside and lead us into the truth of God's Word.

She then talked about the greatest commandment and how Christ talked of love and forgiveness. Victoria spoke on how the enemy uses people and how it's not the person but Satan's spirits using the person to irritate her. She told her about flesh and blood and that we battle principalities and powers in the spirit realm. Lastly, she told her about the armor of God and the purpose of each article.

Gloria soaked up everything Victoria told her and studied every scripture verse. She knew the Holy Spirit was indeed helping her because now when someone would try her, she knew that it was the evil spirit working behind the person. She practiced the Love walk and being obedient when the Holy Spirit would check her. This was working Gloria, thought to herself one day, and she loved it.

At the end of the six weeks, Gloria Santiago and Victoria Hutchinson realized that despite their difference in age, they were no longer client and counselor but they were friends, even sisters. Victoria had begun to introduce Gloria as her little sister and she lovingly called her Niñera (baby sister) too.

In the time she had begun counseling the youth, Victoria had been seeing Reverend Trolli. He had proposed and she accepted. The next year Victoria and Rev. Tee were married and Gloria was her maid of honor. Victoria's son and the rest of her family welcomed Gloria with open arms and they all called her Niñera.

Epilogue

Gloria Maria Santiago
Monday at 9:15am

Since Gloria had landed the receptionist job at the electric company, she enjoyed working as a receptionist because she liked talking. She had become very good at her job and was considered for an administrative assistant position. Gloria was overjoyed when she was given the Admin position.

She was excited with her new job and the changes in her life, however, she knew she needed more on the spiritual side. She loved her newfound relationship with Abba Father and she found that she wanted more and more of Him in her life and she wanted to do something in the church. She had found herself pondering the verse in the Bible about being a doer, and she wanted to do something. **"But be doers of the word, and not hearers only" James 1:22**.

As a result of this new hunger, Gloria had begun working in the children's ministry at church and found that it was fulfilling. She had also started visiting her mother in prison, which had been very hard for Gloria in the beginning. Even with her relationship with God and her hunger for more, the angry spirit would still haunt her, but she was learning to speak God's Word when the attack came.

After she had decided to continue her second set of sessions with Victoria, she learned about forgiveness and being set free through it. Gloria understood and was able to embrace this new knowledge. When she began visiting her mother more often she was able to forgive her and Minister God's love and forgiveness.-Then Gloria led her mother to Christ, repeating the Sinner's Prayer she had learned from Victoria.

Gloria also began the spring trimester at the church Bible College. Gloria Santiago knew and said it often to Victoria and others that she had a long way to go. "But boy oh boy I sure have come a long way from where I used to be." She smiled and Victoria smiled back.

Caleb Jeremiah Austin

Caleb had joined the intercessory prayer team at church and had become involved in the youth basketball league. He was good at basketball and "very smart" the youth minister had said. They asked Caleb if he might be interested in coaching the younger kids and if he might be able to tutor some of them that were falling behind in math. Caleb loved math and wanted to help but he wasn't sure if he had time for the coaching. He had gotten his GED and had applied to take some business courses at the community college. Caleb was interested in becoming an accountant. Since Rev. Tee had been an accounting major he might be willing to help Caleb study while he was learning accounting. Caleb knew that he would have to study; and with his part-time job and chores at the farm, he didn't want to take on more than he could handle. Miss Rose and Mr. Mike were still letting him stay even though he had turned seventeen and could be on his own. Mr. Mike had said he could use Caleb's help around the farm and he would be a help to the other foster children and their homework. Caleb would pray about everything he had to do and all of his decisions; up on that rooftop with Abba Father had become his favorite place to be.

Although he didn't get to spend nearly as much time as he used to at the community center, he still went to see Rev. Tee as often as possible. They would talk about God and all of the things Caleb was involved in. Rev. Tee, Mr. Mike, Miss Rose and Miss Victoria always encouraged him and they told him how proud of him they were. This made him happy. He knew he wasn't "sorry" and he would often look up and say, "Mom you were so right, someone up there does love me and I'm already a success in His eyes."

Vincent Anthony Incorvia

Vincent had joined the witnessing team and was getting more people saved than anyone else. He had a zeal and a passion for people to know Christ. He had begun taking the full course of study in correspondence and had been made assistant foreman at work after the Assistant foreman who harassed him was fired for stealing bread.

Vincent only had six months of parole left to do. He wanted to become a Bible school teacher at the local church. Celeste was so proud of her son Vincent and she never called him Vinnie again. She and Vincent Sr. were now divorced. He had moved out of town and Celeste had moved on with her life. She was also taking classes to become a nurse, which had been a lifelong dream. Vincent encouraged his mom and she encouraged him. Victoria encouraged them both so Vincent had decided to keep going to counseling with her. Even though Celeste was far beyond the ages Victoria normally worked with she was able to counsel her as well. Victoria also took on some other adults but only saw them once a month. She continued counseling more young people once a week as this was her lifelong dream.

Vincent said to Victoria, "You know, I used to always say, I gotta get myself together so I'm so glad I finally learned that I needed God to get me together." Vincent eventually met and married Sally Abbott. Sally was a Bible school teacher dedicated to God and Kingdom work; she also was a wonderful help to Vincent, she encouraged him daily. Vincent loved Sally with all his heart; she was second only to beloved Abba Father.

Stephanie LaTrese Davis

Stephanie finished her time in physical rehabilitation, while attending Narcotics Anonymous (N.A.) meetings. She was doing quite well. She had a new sponsor who also was an adamant believer. Stephanie, Mable and Victoria had gone to get restraining orders against Rick. The relationship between mother and daughter had grown stronger with God in charge and Victoria's assistance. Stephanie and Mable had also gone to get Stephanie's children and later had them dedicated to God, with a vow to raise them in the nurture and admonition of Him. Mable and Stephanie had both become great friends with Charity Livingston; they also joined her Bible study group on Thursday nights.

When the court dates for Rick came up Mable, Victoria, Stephanie, Charity and a host of doctors, nurses and police officers were there to testify against him. Rick was sentenced to seven to twelve years in the state penitentiary, charged for attempted murder also for the charge of stalking with intent to cause harm. He also had two cases pending for drug possession and trafficking. Oh yes, Richard Rowlands would be looking out through bars for many years to come. All the women, including Mable and Stephanie, prayed that he would find Christ and be delivered.

Mable now had a job as an accounts payable clerk for the church, thanks to her background in accounting and the years of keeping that restaurant going; Charity Livingston's reference didn't hurt either. Stephanie was able to start school at the state college and her course of study was elementary education.

Richard (Rick) Rowlings
The Gentleman's Club that Richard "Rick" Rowlings owned was raided; upward of thirty kilos of cocaine was found in Rick's office along with five pounds of marijuana bagged, bricks of more and baggies with crack and a large assortment of prescription pills. There were stacks of cash that amounted to more than $180,000 in a safe. The club was engaged in prostitution, trafficking, drugs, and many other illegal activities. Rick was also convicted on those charges and wouldn't see the light of day for many years to come.

Aidan Hunter O'Connor
Aidan continued listening for God's voice for everything he did. He also knew that his calling was to be a Christian counselor. He set out to finish school and study behavioral health while he was still in high school. There happened to be some night classes that he could take even at his age and they would be a big help to him as far as credits go when he got to college.

Now that Aidan could hear Abba's voice again, he had forgotten all about being angry with his dad and other people until one day he went to the mall and he saw Paul in the parking lot. Paul was a complete bum. He was actually pan handling. He had on tattered dirty sneakers and old clothes that looked a size and a half too big. Aidan walked near where Paul stood and he smelled of sweat and alcohol and he had a ragged beard and mustache. "Dad," Aidan spoke out; when Paul turned to look at his son, he smiled. Aidan saw that his teeth were rotted and a few were missing. Immediately Paul said, "Hey boy you got any money for your ole dad?"

Aidan turned to run. "I ran and ran until I couldn't run anymore," When he told Victoria about his encounter, he said "Who was that man?" 'I wanted to hate him, I wanted to scream at him, I wanted to punch him out, but all I could do was run and cry," Aidan said sadly." "What is this Miss Victoria? What am I supposed to do?" he asked with fresh tears in his eyes. Victoria felt tears stinging the backs of her eyelids, but she resisted the urge to let them fall. Aidan needed her strength now, he needed Christ's strength. She told Aidan about Reverend Trolli and the youth center and she knew he could help. She knew how well Rev. Tee had related to Caleb. Rev. Tee had helped many boys who had been rejected. Besides his accounting, he too had background in behavioral science. She would set up a meeting. One thing Victoria knew was that Aidan needed a strong male influence in his life just as Caleb had. Now Aidan would listen for God's voice and he also had the mortal and moral guidance of a sensitive yet stern, understanding man who wore many hats.

With Rev. Tee's help Aidan would eventually fulfill his dream. He was able to forgive and talk with Paul but Paul refused to help himself or to go into a rehab center. Finally, Paul told Aidan that he had been diagnosed with stage four pancreatic cancer. Aidan would visit Paul in the boarding house for the next year until one day on his sixteenth birthday he got the call that his dad had begun to transition. When Aiden arrived, he spoke to Paul and went through the prayer of repentance. Paul accepted Christ and forgiveness and within ten minutes of Aidan's prayer, Paul was gone.

Aidan never really heard from or saw his mother. He guessed it was because he looked a lot like his dad Paul. He had looked for her once and he even got close to seeing her. He found out her phone number from one of her old friends but when he called the number, she had told him that she thought it would be best if they didn't get together. Just like that, his mother wanted no part of him. To his surprise, he didn't feel hurt, just a little sad for her. He never really knew her anyway. Aidan decided to just keep her in prayer and love her from afar.

Rev. Tee and Ms. Victoria had become like parents to him and he was fine with that. He figured as long as Abba continues to talk to me, I'll be alright. He had settled on and decided he would just continue to pray that someone would cross his mom's path and lead her to Christ. "Who knows what the future holds but the Most High God?" Aidan thought to himself and prayed, "Father, Your ways and thoughts are higher than mine so I trust You with my Mom and I leave it all with You, in Christ's name Amen." He left it right there and went on with his life.

Victoria

Victoria continued her work as the church's behavioral counselor to youth. During the next years she would have many encounters with many troubled youth with drama-filled lives. With some she was successful and with others she was only able to plant the seed and pray that it be watered so that God could give the increase in the understanding of Him and increase their lives to fulfill their potential. God's plan is to increase them with everything that pertains to life and godliness as told in **2 Peter 1:3**. In the meantime, she would always prophecy to their dry bones.

Victoria loved her job and her missionary work with her new husband, Reverend Tee, whom she loved dearly. Most of all she loved Abba Father more and more as she continued in her destiny. This was her dream she had heard the call of God and she had answered. She would continue to "Walk Among Dry Bones" and prophesy the Good News.

"Also I heard the voice of the Most High, saying: 'Whom shall I send, and who will go for Us?' Then I said, 'Here am I! Send me.'" Isaiah 6:8

God's Grace Abounds

Inspired by Psalm 61:3 and written by Cynthia Atkinson

Many times, trials come to confuse us
at times things seem so bleak.
These are the times that we must focus
and know God's promise is complete.
He'll walk us through the trials of life
when all is stormy and nothing seems bright.
Trust in God and the power of His might,
His promise is to see us through every plight.
He'll be our refuge and strong tower
then from within us will flow His power.
And when it seems He's far away
He shows Himself stronger each and every day.
And when life's cares spin you 'round and 'round
remember God's grace will always abound.

To my Dear Readers

This book is based on some fictional and some non-fictional accounts from my heart. With it comes added imagery to help the reader visualize the supernatural components of this book.

Further, I ask if you can identify with any of the character's challenges or if you have struggles that aren't mentioned in the book but that keep you from having a good life. If so I can assure you that the God (Jesus) discussed in this book can help you just as He helped those in this book as well as myself. Whatever it may be it all takes time and it is a process. Life will still be full of challenges but the Holy Spirit will help you, just as He helped Gloria, Stephanie, Caleb, Aidan and Vincent.

With that said, if you haven't yet accepted Christ as your Savior, I would like to take this opportunity to invite you, to invite Him into your life and heart? If your answer is yes I would love to lead you in a prayer of salvation and acceptance of Christ as Lord of your life.

Prayer

Dear Heavenly Father. I am coming to you today to ask You to come into my heart, I know that I have been a sinner but now I believe that Christ died for me to have a better more abundant life. I thank You for forgiving me of my sin and for coming into my heart and I thank You in advance for guiding me daily. Amen

Now that you have accepted Christ into your heart, I would like to be the first to welcome you into the family, and to make a few suggestions. I recommend that you find a good local church to attend. If I may, I also propose that you look for a few good on-line pastors that are known as good teachers, who can explain Biblical concepts well.

These are a couple of Online teaching ministries that I know of; Bishop Derek Grier, Grace Church, Dumfries VA and Bishop B. Courtney McBath the Senior Pastor of Calvary Revival Church (CRC) in Norfolk, Virginia, both are very good teachers and are easy to follow and they explain things well.

Thank you all for taking this journey with me as we are all
Walking Among Dry Bones

Scripture references taken from New King James, SFL Version Bible, Amplified and Awakening's Hebrew Scripture

About The Author

Cynthia Atkinson is a native of Erie, Pennsylvania and is the ninth child of a family of twelve children. She is the mother of three children and has many grandchildren and six great-grandchildren.

Cynthia moved to Richmond, Virginia in 1996 following a call to ministry where she later began attending Bible College. As A 2004 Honors Graduate Of Faith Landmark Bible Institute, Cynthia endeavored to get an even better understanding of the Word of God by returning to FLBI and serving as a teacher's assistant for five years.

She consecutively and faithfully served five years in the juvenile prison ministry but before this, she was an altar worker and choir member at Faith Landmarks Ministries where she was a member for eighteen years.

While living in Richmond, Cynthia also served as the Editor in Chief for the Women Empowering Women Newsletter (WEWN a division of Women of Power Prayer and Presence Fellowship Inc., Located in Henrico, Virginia). She is also an inspirational writer, teacher, singer and songwriter/composer of Christian music.

Cynthia has returned to her native town of Erie, PA where she continues in juvenile & women's prison ministry. She is now in the process of working on her second book as she continues to pursue other spiritual and literary projects. As always, she continues her commitment to building God's kingdom.

To Contact The Publishing Company

Are you interested in writing or having your work (book, manuscript, poetry, how-to-do, autobiography/biography, etc.) published? Then reach out to the publishing company. We provide an array of consulting and publishing services.

Crown And Cross Consulting And Publishing Co LLC
Attention: Kimberly Stratton – CEO and Founder
PO Box 952607
Lake Mary, FL 32795
Email: thecrownandcrosspublishingco@outlook.com

Notes

www.ingramcontent.com/pod-product-compliance
Lightning Source LLC
Chambersburg PA
CBHW071211160426
43196CB00011B/2255